To

MAURA SULLIVAN

1st Lt. - USMC;

U.S. MARINE,

WARRIOR,

&

AMERICAN PATRIOT.

SEMPER FI!

Vincent F. Stanbury

28 OCTOBER 2003

This book is a gift from
LtGen. Chuck Pitman

Warrior Culture
of the
U.S. Marines

Axioms for Warriors,
Marine Quotations, Battle History,
Reflections on Combat, Corps Legacy,
Humor - *and much more* - for
the World's Warrior Elite

Marion F. Sturkey

Heritage Press International

Warrior Culture of the U.S. Marines

Second Edition
-- First printing: February 2002
-- Second printing: November 2003

Library of Congress Control Number: 2003111168

ISBN: 0-9650814-1-9

Heritage Press International
204 Jefferson Street
P.O. Box 333
Plum Branch, SC 29845 USA

Manufactured in the United States of America

Acknowledgements

Grateful acknowledgement is extended to each American Patriot who has *earned the title*, United States Marine. They have made this project possible. Since the birth of their Corps in 1775, these warriors have epitomized the virtues of Honor, Courage, and Commitment. Through their unequalled prowess in combat, their undying loyalty to Corps and Country, and their selfless sacrifices for fellow Marines, they have erected to themselves and to their Corps a monument more enduring than marble.

Further, grateful acknowledgement is extended to the hundreds of United States Marines who, without thought of recognition or reward, contributed to the content of this project.

Further, grateful acknowledgement is extended to Headquarters United States Marine Corps for permission to use the U.S. Marine Corps Emblem, as depicted herein, and for technical assistance in this regard.

Further, grateful acknowledgement is extended to the United States Marine Corps Recruiting Command for assistance in regard to the USMC Recruiting Posters and other material depicted herein.

Table of Contents

Part One embraces Marine Corps history and the Warrior Culture of the Corps. Readers will find everything from Tun Tavern to *The Marines' Hymn* -- a treasure trove for all American Patriots who have *earned the title*.

Part Two offers *Happy Hour* fare for U.S. Marines. Yet, Marines find wisdom in these jocular proverbs. Those who ignore these timeless truths of combat do so at their own peril.

-- Part One --

(continued on next page)

-- Part Two --

Heads-up for Nitpickers

Military Abbreviations: Continental Army? French Army? Luftwaffe? Imperial Japanese Navy? Such infrequently referenced military services are identified in full in this book. However, more frequently referenced military services are identified by abbreviations. After a warrior's rank and name, the following abbreviations identify the branch of service:

USMC	United States Marine Corps
USA	United States Army
USN	United States Navy
USAF	United States Air Force
CSMC	Confederate States Marine Corps
CSA	Confederate States Army
CSN	Confederate States Navy
RN	Royal Navy (British)
RAF	Royal Air Force (British)

Commandant of the Marine Corps: The Commandant of the Marine Corps ranks below The Deity -- but *not very far* below. When a statement is credited to the Commandant, the designation "(CMC)" will follow. For example, a handwritten note penned by the Commandant in 1836 is credited: "Col. Archibald Henderson, USMC (CMC)." A statement voiced by the Commandant in 1997 is credited: "Gen. Charles C. Krulak, USMC (CMC)."

Military Rank: A warrior's military rank may be shown as Corporal in one instance, and as Sergeant in a later instance. The person's rank *at the time of the event* is used. Daniel J. "Dan" Daly was a hard-charging USMC Private when he garnered his first Medal of Honor, and a crusty old Gunnery Sergeant when he got his second such award 15 years later. Lewis B. "Chesty" Puller

(continued on next page)

was a vocal USMC Colonel in Korea, but an even more outspoken Lieutenant General before the end of the decade.

Civilian Sources: The title, position, or "claim to fame" of civilian sources is stated when known, for example: (1) U.S. Senator, (2) war correspondent, (3) draft dodger, (4) British Prime Minister, (5) German historian, etc.

On Active Duty? Once a Marine, Always a Marine! A gung-ho USMC Master Sergeant first made that famous statement during a tavern argument. He was right on target.

This book makes no distinction between (1) Marines on active duty, (2) Marine reservists, (3) Marine veterans, (4) Marine retirees, etc. Once the title, United States Marine, has been earned, it is retained forever. The single badge of honor, **"USMC,"** identifies *all* lifelong members of the elite Brotherhood of Marines.

Gender? There is only one kind of United States Marine, the fighting kind. Gender? Who knows? Who cares?

The Corps is always on the lookout for "A Few Good Men." Recently, the Corps has kept its eyes peeled for "A Few Good Women," too. Each individual Marine, man or woman, has *earned the title*. Each is a proud patriot, a Marine Warrior.

With respect to gender, this book contains no "politically correct" psycho-babble. Readers will find no "he or she" foolishness or "him or her" lunacy. The male pronoun suffices for all. Any pitiful wimps who dislike this storied Warrior Culture ethos should find something else to read.

-- military books by Marion Sturkey --

BONNIE-SUE: A Marine Corps Helicopter Squadron in Vietnam:
(first published in 1996) Professional, 21 photographs, 4 maps. A
timeless best-selling classic. Often considered the definitive work
on Marine Corps helicopter warfare in Vietnam. Yet, the book
soars high above the mud of war. The author blends emotion,
detail, and grim realism. He breathes life into a daily struggle for
survival. Against the backdrop of the turbulent 1960s, *BONNIE-
SUE'* evolves into a riveting saga of commitment and sacrifice,
love and brotherhood. No profanity.

Warrior Culture of the U.S. Marines: (first published in 2002)
Axioms for Warriors, Marine Quotations, USMC Battle History,
Reflections on Combat, Corps Legacy -- and much more -- for the
world's warrior elite. Everything you ever wanted to know about
America's premier fighting force. Plus, plenty of *satire* exclusively
for U.S. Marines. Totally gung-ho! Up-beat! "Politically Incorrect" and proud of it. The ultimate book for Marine Warriors,
the modern-day American Samurai. No profanity.

Murphy's Laws of Combat: (first published in 2003) A walk on
the humorous side of military life. Military satire for all branches
of the U.S. Armed Forces. Politically Impossible! Hundreds of
up-beat *tongue-in-cheek* combat laws, principles, and axioms. Plus,
profit from Murphy's rules of sex & seduction, Murphy's beer-
drinking guide, Murphy's principles of stupidity, and much more.
Also, military quotations and the American military heritage. This
is the book for warriors (or warrior wannabes), young and old, who
enjoy a good laugh -- usually at themselves. No profanity.

Heritage Press International
204 Jefferson Street
P.O. Box 333
Plum Branch, SC 29845 USA
    Phone: 864-443-5081
    Fax: 864-443-5572
    E-mail: MarionS@wctel.net
    Web Site: **www.USMCpress.com**

for all
American Patriots
who have
earned the title,
United States Marine

PART ONE

Warrior Culture of the U.S. Marines

Some people spend an entire lifetime wondering if they made a difference in the world. But, the Marines don't have that problem! [Ronald Reagan, U.S. President, 1985]

U.S. Marines, the American Samurai

Leathernecks or Jarheads! Devil Dogs, Gyrenes, or whatever! By any name, the world recognizes U.S. Marines as the premier warriors on planet Earth.

Marines have evolved into American icons, the Warrior Elite. Why? What makes them tick? What is the Marine Corps? And why does the individual Marine stand head and shoulders above all of the world's warrior wannabes?

The answers are complex. True, the Marine Corps is a military force, but it is much more. The Corps is an elite fraternity, a spiritual brotherhood. Entry is a *calling*. For most, *earning the title* is closely akin to becoming a priest. Yet, the ethos of the Warrior Culture of the Marines is simple: ***prowess in combat***.

Each U.S. Marine, past and present, has entered more than just the Brotherhood of Marines. He has become, and always will remain, part of a mystical fellowship of valor. He must comply with hallowed rituals. He must conform to an uncompromising code of honor, discipline, and personal integrity. Commitment to his Corps -- that is right, *his* Corps -- and moral strength become the norm. Throughout the history of the Corps these virtues have sustained Marine Warriors during the chaos of combat.

Marines remain a breed apart. Each Marine draws strength from his Corps. In return, the strength and legacy of the Marine Corps lie in the collective *will* of each individual Marine. The Corps glories in a tradition of service and sacrifice. In their unique Corps, grown men speak openly of their brotherly love for fellow Marines whom they have never met. They share a bond, a love, a dedication and loyalty that no earthly circumstance can shatter. It is *their* Corps, *their* elite Brotherhood of Marines!

Yet, in today's "politically correct" and technological world, some outsiders now question the time-honored traditions of the

Marine Corps. Are the Marines *visionaries*? Or, *lunatics*? Have the Marines drifted out of control? Out of touch? Are they too extreme in practice and attitude?

Many critics believe that the Marines are culturally outdated, clinging to the principles of Teddy Roosevelt and unwilling to accept change. Why, these critics wonder, do Marines still speak of *loyalty*, *honor*, and *patriotism* -- words rarely heard in school classrooms these days? Critics also point out that Marines speak of their Commandant with almost the same degree of reverence accorded to The Deity. Why?

Many outsiders often scoff that the Marines just do not seem to fit in, do not seem to follow the crowd. Nay-sayers note that when songs of other military services (*Anchors Aweigh*, *The Army Goes Rolling Along*, and *Off We Go into the Wild Blue Yonder*) are played in public, advocates jump for joy, shout, cheer, and jive to the music. Scoffers quickly note that the Marines are different. First of all, they do not even have a song. Instead, they have a *hymn*. And when *The Marines' Hymn* is played, Marines do not clap their hands or cheer. Instead, they stand at attention, silent and mute. Is there something horribly wrong with this picture?

One psychologist claims that most Marines are mentally unstable, irrational, dangerous. Their "gungy" verbiage is foolish, he reports. From his point of view the Marines are too stubborn, too haughty, too mischievous, too obsessed with weapons and violence. The alarmed psychologist notes that Marines habitually make uncivilized animal noises and grunt their silly *"Ooo-rah!"* They laugh when nothing is funny. They relish the moniker, "Uncle Sam's Misguided Children." The somber verdict of the civilian psychologist: "They're a bunch of nuts."

Without question, the Marines are truly obsessed. Why, many outsiders wonder, do the Marines need to have a *creed* for almost everything? The Corps has a *Rifleman's Creed*, an *NCO Creed*, a *Staff NCO Creed*, a *Drill Instructor's Creed*, and on and on and on. The Marines even have *The Marine's Prayer*, of all things.

Are the Marines truly trapped in an archaic out-of-date time warp? Today, does America still need the U.S. Marine Corps?

The Marines agree. They *are* different. Different, as in *better!* The Marine Corps gets only six cents from each Department of

Defense dollar. But for that six cents, America gets the most lethal fighting force the world has ever known. The U.S. Marines are respected by America's friends and feared by her foes.

Alone among the American military services, the elite Marine Corps retains gender separation in basic training -- for outsiders, that is **warrior training**. And while the Army, Air Force, and Navy recruiters tell prospective recruits what the military can offer them (travel, college tuition, benefits, etc.), the Marines remain silent. They make no offers. Instead, Marine recruiters have two simple questions: "What do you have to offer our Corps?" and "What makes you think you can become a Marine?"

Among the American military services, only the elite Marine Corps mandates a Professional Reading List. In the Corps, privates and sergeants, lieutenants and colonels, all must do their required reading. **Extreme?** Yes! **Tough?** Yes! The Marines do more with less, and they like it that way.

Over the years the U.S. Marines have garnered the meanest mascot, the English Bulldog; the best fighting knife, the Ka-Bar; the most rigorous boot camps and OCS; their own digitized battle cammies (copyrighted, no less); and the best motivational shout, "Ooo-rah!" Further, those raggedy you-know-what Marines relish their unique phone number, 1-800-MARINES; their most dashing uniforms, Dress Blues; their best recruiting station, Tun Tavern; their unique sniper rifles, .50 caliber ("get some"); their Marine Recons, the *stealth* version of the basic Marine Grunt; and their Drill Instructors, the meanest and toughest warriors who ever walked upon the face of the Earth.

In many ways the Marines *are* old-fashioned. They salute their country's flag. They take the *Pledge of Allegiance* to heart. Surrounded by a civilian "me-first" and "every-man-for-himself" world, they still emphasize old-fashioned teamwork. Marines also know the legacy of their Corps. They know that whenever the President of the United States flies in a helicopter, he is flying in "Marine One." They know that at any American Embassy on the planet, the guards are U.S. Marines. And they surely know that back in 1962, Col. John H. Glenn Jr., USMC, was the first American astronaut to orbit the earth -- and that he did it *again* 36 years later at age 77. The Marines! The elite!

Marines revere their heroes, their legends. In the Corps the heroes are genuine *battle* heroes, not just some paper-pushing efficiency experts, library assistants, mail clerks, or staff pogues. Chesty Puller enlisted as a Marine recruit. He lived to fight, loved to fight, loved his Corps. Chesty rose to Lieutenant General, and along the way was awarded the Navy Cross *five* times. Today in Marine boot camp, just before *lights out*, the recruits must solemnly intone: "Goodnight, Chesty, wherever you are!"

Chesty is not alone. Smedley Butler, Dan Daly, "Manila John" Basilone, and legions of other Marines dedicated their lives to Corps and Country. On battlefields around the globe they gutted it out with the discipline, courage, prowess, and leadership needed to survive and win in combat. The Warrior Culture!

Yes, the Marine Corps does not fit in. The Army has *soldiers*. The Navy has *sailors*. The Air Force has *airmen* or *zoomies* or whatever. But only the combat oriented Marines have bestowed the name of their Corps upon each member of their brotherhood, regardless of rank. The Marine Corps has *Marines*. Each Marine is an integral part of his Corps. He *is* the Corps. Marines and their Corps are inseparable, they are one. The U.S. Marines!

Marine Corps training is longer, harder, more demanding, and tailored for the demands of combat. Marines relish their point-of-the-spear role. Their Warrior Culture demands nothing less. The Marines assault, conquer, and then go home, leaving the occupation chores to the Army. And when their Country calls, the Marines go armed to the teeth with their Marine Corps "*Air Force*." Marine Air, as Marines call it, flies fixed wing transports, fighters, ground attack aircraft, and helicopters (standing alone, Marine Air would be the eighth largest *Air Force* in the world). The Marines have three Air Wings, one to complement each of their three Marine Divisions, plus another Air Wing and Division in the reserves. This lethal combination springs from a congressional mandate, the National Security Act of 1947, as amended.

The Marines have Armor, Artillery, Marine Air, and a host of supporting arms. Coordinated by a dizzying array of hi-tech electronics, the Corps packs a devastating punch. Yet, despite all the lethality and sophistication, the most basic tenet of Marine Corps doctrine remains the Marine infantryman, the **Magnificent Grunt**. Even the U.S. Army has acknowledged: "The deadliest weapon in the world is a Marine and his rifle." In the Marine

Corps, all revolves around the Grunt, the rifleman. Every Marine, whether he is a fighter jet pilot or a tank commander, was first trained as a rifleman, a Grunt.

If you want fighting slogans, the Corps has them: *First to Fight! Once a Marine, Always a Marine! Death before Dishonor! A Few Good Men!* There are many more (see the sub-chapter, "Selected Marine Corps Slogans and Sayings"). What outsiders often fail to realize is that these slogans are actually statements of fact. In the Corps these time-honored truisms are more than mere slogans. They are a way of life, words to live by, words to fight by.

And, *fighting* is what Marines do best: the Mexican War (the halls of Montezuma), the Barbary Wars (the shores of Tripoli), and the Florida Indian Wars, where the *Commandant* led his Marines into battle. And after that: the Boxer Rebellion, Haiti, Belleau Wood, and the Argonne. In World War II: Guadalcanal, Tarawa, Peleliu, Iwo Jima, and Okinawa. More recently: Chosin Reservoir, Khe Sanh, Hue City, Kuwait, Afghanistan, and Iraq.

Bracketing the beginning of the Third Millennium, the Marines played the pivotal role in two wars in the Middle East.

1991: Kuwait, then occupied by the Iraqi Army, had been bombarded by air for weeks. By late February a half-million coalition combatants stood ready to liberate Kuwait. The vast majority would ride across hundreds of miles of undefended desert in a "left hook." But first they would wait on the world's warrior elite, the U.S. Marines.

As usual, the Marines formed the point of the spear. Instead of undefended desert, they faced the teeth of the Iraqi defenses. They would have to fight their way through the Iraqi *wall of death*: row upon row of fire trenches, berms, minefields, tank barricades, and tens of thousands of dug-in defenders.

The Iraqis planned to *channel* the Marines into "killing zones" targeted by thousands of 300mm rockets and 1,200 artillery pieces (the same slaughterhouse tactic that Iraq had used, along with poison gas, to decimate hundreds of thousands of Iranian soldiers in the previous decade). The Iraqi plan was no secret. MGen. Mike Myatt, USMC, bluntly stated: "We knew the Iraqis were planning on trapping us in *'fire sacks.'*"

Nonetheless, despite the lethal odds against them, the audacious

Marines would attack. The rest of the coalition would wait. Then, when all of the Iraqi might and fury was focused upon annihilating the remaining Marines, the unopposed "left hook" could begin.

Before dawn on 24 February 1991 the locked and loaded warriors of the 1st and 2nd Marine Divisions waited. Without warning at 0400 hours -- at mega-decibel levels -- their psyops loudspeakers shattered the quiet of the night with *The Marines' Hymn*. Led by their tanks and bulldozers on the ground, and with Marine Air swarming overhead, the Marines stormed the Iraqi defenses.

Within minutes the only sound was a continuous deafening cacophony from exploding artillery, rockets, mines, line-charges, and the wail of jet turbines. Marines blasted and fought their way through the firestorm at the defensive line. Then, waiting for them behind the *wall of death* were hundreds of Iraqi tanks and six more Iraqi infantry divisions.

In the Burquan oil field the Corps fought the largest tank battle in its history. Marines on the ground and Marine Air left hundreds of burning enemy tanks behind as they battled their way northward. At Kuwait International Airport the Corps reduced another 320 enemy tanks to burning hulks -- 1,042 total enemy tanks destroyed.

By the evening of the second day the hard-charging U.S. Marines had blasted their way to the outskirts of Kuwait City. With them was LtGen. Walter Boomer, USMC, in his command-and-control variant LAV. Here the victorious Marines stopped, for their battle was over. Their Arab allies would be given the honor of rolling into the now-undefended capital city.

2003: For twelve years an armed and belligerent Iraq, under the heel of a maniacal tyrant, had thumbed its nose at the rest of the civilized world. In response to an international appeal the United States led a coalition to end the reign of terror and the military threat to the world community.

On 20 March 2003 the warriors of the First Marine Expeditionary Force prepared to charge into battle. To a man, they were eager to test themselves under fire, eager to close with the enemy, eager to fight for Corps and Country. "This is the best day of my life!" shouted 1stLt. Patrick S. Henry, USMC, as he and his brothers-in-arms loaded up at the ammunition supply point.

Another U.S. Marine, SSgt. Wallace M. Mains, loaded down with ammo, grinned and exclaimed: "It's showtime!"

The Marines stormed north from their staging area in Kuwait. They charged into the fabled "cradle of civilization," ancient Mesopotamia, the heartland of Iraq between the Tigris and Euphrates Rivers. Racing through the Rumeila oil fields, within hours they captured the crucial port city of Umm Qasr.

North of Umm Qasr the Iraqi Army decided to stand and fight. Bad decision! The mobility, firepower, and 'elan of the Marine Warriors overwhelmed the Iraqi defenders at Afaq, Diwaniya, Al Kut, and countless other cities on the road to the Iraqi capital. Even the firestorm at "Ambush Valley" in Nasiriyah failed to stop the Marine onslaught. Backed by Marine Air, the Grunts shot and blasted their way through the enemy infantry and armor. Brute force, firepower, and Marine tradition prevailed. Viewing the destruction two days later, Capt. James A. Smith, the U.S. Army liaison officer, would exclaim in awe: "The [expletive] Marines have killed every living thing except the snakes and lizards!"

By 7 April 2003 the Marine juggernaut had destroyed all enemy opposition along the 350-mile line of attack. Marine Warriors had fought their way to the gates of Baghdad. Through a barrage of enemy fire they attacked across the Diyala Bridge, closed to belly-ripping bayonet range, annihilated the opposing "death squads," and then fanned out into the city. As the world watched on live television, a Marine armored vehicle toppled the massive statue of Saddam Hussein in Al Fridos Square on 9 April. After this symbolic triumph, enemy resistance soon faded away.

During the last week of the war the Marines -- who get only *6 percent* of each Department of Defense dollar -- earned *53 percent* of the embedded media TV war coverage. Next the Leathernecks found and rescued the seven Army soldiers who had been held as POWs. Then they gave Baghdad to the Army for occupation.

Once again, as they have done since 1775, Marine Warriors proved that when success in battle is the need, the Brotherhood of Marines is the right answer. The revered warriors of the U.S. Marine Corps remain the modern-day American Samurai, the most lethal fighting machine on planet Earth.

Throughout the ages, all who have *earned the title* live forever in this immortal band of brothers. They are America's Patriots. ***Always Faithful! The Few! The Proud! The Marines!***

Marine Corps Legacy
(from *admirers,* and a few *enemies*)

Any fool can toot his own horn. It means nothing. Any self-serving dolt can praise himself. Again, it means nothing.

The true measure of greatness lies in the collective opinion of others. Excellence never goes unnoticed. Spontaneous praise and respect from others in-the-know remain the time tested benchmarks for military professionalism and combat prowess.

Praise? The Marine Corps gets it! *Respect?* Marine Warriors have it! In the Corps, respect and praise are a way of life.

Below are accolades that *others* have heaped upon U.S. Marines and their Corps. This praise comes from foreign statesmen, U.S. presidents, historians, and combat correspondents. Further tributes come from other branches of the United States armed forces, the Air Force and the Navy. But most such praise comes from soldiers in the U.S. Army. Soldiers recognize true battlefield excellence when they see Marine Warriors in combat.

Praise and respect also come from military *adversaries* who have tangled with U.S. Marines in combat. These adversaries know the Marine Corps better than anyone else on earth. To their chagrin, they have tasted the fighting prowess of Marine Warriors.

So, let us hear it from the mouths of others, from the unbiased outsiders. They are the objective experts. In their words, here is the Marine Corps Legacy:

I should not deem a man-of-war complete without a body of Marines.
[Commodore Joshua R. Sands, USN; in a letter, 1852]

The Marines will never disappoint the most sanguine expectations of their country -- never! I have never known one who would not readily advance in battle.
[Capt. C.W. Morgan, USN; in a letter, 1852]

The Marines are at all times prompt in the execution of any duty.
[Col. Robert E. Lee, USA (*prior* to the American Civil War); after the capture of abolitionist John Brown, 18 October 1859]

A ship without Marines is like a garment without buttons.
[RAdm. David D. Porter, USN; in a letter, 1863]

If the Marines are abolished, half the efficiency of the Navy will be destroyed.
[RAdm. David D. Porter, USN; in a letter, 6 December 1863]

It gives me pleasure to report to you the fine bearing and soldierly conduct of Captain Wilson and his Marines.
[Cmdr. J. Taylor Wood, CSN; praising the Confederate States Marines led by Capt. Thomas Wilson, CSMC; 16 February 1864]

There is the finest body of troops in the world, those gallant Marines who are ever ready to devote themselves to the interests of their country.
[Benjamin Disraeli, Prime Minister of England; 1879]

The Marines have landed and the situation is well in hand.
[Richard H. Davis, war correspondent; Panama, 1885]

No finer military organization than the Marine Corps exists in the world.
[Adm. George Dewey, USN; in a letter, 1898]

To our Marines fell the most difficult and dangerous portion of the defense by reason of our proximity to the great city wall and the main city gate . . . The Marines acquitted themselves nobly.
[Edwin N. Conger, U.S. Minister; Peking, China, 1900]

There is no military body in our country of higher efficiency than the Marine Corps. They take great pride in their profession.
[RAdm. C.M. Winslow, USN; to the U.S. Congress, 1916]

I am convinced there is no smarter, handier, or more adaptable

body of troops in the world.
  [Winston Churchill, writing about the U.S. Marines, 1917]

Why in hell can't the Army do it if the Marines can? They are the
same kind of men; why can't they be like Marines?
  [Gen. John J. "Black Jack" Pershing, USA; 12 February 1918]

In a hundred and fifty years they [U.S. Marines] have never been
beaten. They will hold.
  [Col. Preston Brown, USA; speaking of the Marine regiment
  replacing the routed French units in a desperate last-ditch effort
  to stop the German advance on Paris, June 1918]

Their fiery advance and great tenacity were well recognized by
their opponents.
  [LtCol. Ernst Otto, German Army; writing of the repeated U.S.
  Marine onslaughts in Belleau Wood, France, June 1918]

The American Marines are terribly reckless fellows. They would
make very good storm troopers.
  [German Army report from Belleau Wood, France, June 1918]

Let me express the intense admiration, which I share with all other
Americans, of the record made by the Marines.
  [Theodore Roosevelt, former U.S. President; 17 October 1918]

The name of the Marne [in France] will always be associated with
that of the glorious American Marines.
  [Gaston Libert, French Consul General; 1918]

No one can ever say that the Marines have failed to do their work
in handsome fashion.
  [MGen. Johnson Hagood, USA; *Can We Defend America*, 1937]

Dan Daly will live forever as a hero, a legend, a two time Medal
of Honor winner, and as a United States Marine.
  [the text on a memorial in Glen Cove, NY, the hometown of
  SgtMaj. Daniel J. "Dan" Daly (1873-1937), USMC]

Since 1775 the United States Marines have upheld a fine tradition of service to their country.

[Franklin D. Roosevelt, U.S. President; 10 November 1942]

And when he gets to Heaven,
To St. Peter he will tell:
"One more Marine reporting, Sir --
I've served my time in Hell."

[tombstone epitaph of PFC William Cameron, USMC (H/2/1); KIA near Lunga Point on Guadalcanal, Solomon Islands, in the South Pacific, 1942]

They are quite brave.

[a Japanese staff officer, describing the victorious U.S. Marines on Guadalcanal, in a dispatch to Tokyo, 4 March 1943]

Guadalcanal is no longer merely the name of an island. It is the name of the graveyard of the Japanese Army.

[MGen. Kiyotake Kawaguchi, Imperial Japanese Army; in 1943, after U.S. Marines on Guadalcanal handed the Imperial Japanese Army its first defeat in over 1000 years]

Before [the U.S. Marines] are through with them, the Japanese language will be spoken only in Hell.

[Adm. William F. "Bull" Halsey, USN; 1943]

Some 2000 or 3000 United States Marines, most of them now dead or wounded, gave the nation a name to stand beside those of Concord Bridge, the *Bonhomme Richard*, the Alamo, the Little Big Horn, and Belleau Wood. The name was Tarawa. *[and also]* The Marines fought almost solely on *esprit de corps*, I was certain.

[Robert Sherrod, *Time Magazine* correspondent; November 1943]

Whip these Germans so we can get out to the Pacific to kick the [expletive] out of the [expletive] Japanese -- before the [expletive] *Marines* get all the credit!

[Gen. George S. Patton Jr., USA; speaking to the soldiers of his Third Army, in England, 5 June 1944]

The raising of that flag on Suribachi means a Marine Corps for the next five hundred years.
    [James Forrestal, Secretary of the Navy (the flag-raising on Iwo Jima had been immortalized in a photograph by Associated Press photographer Joe Rosenthal); 23 February 1945]

In the Army, shock troops are a small minority supported by a vast group of artisans, laborers, clerks, and organizers. In the Marines, there are practically *nothing but* shock troops.
    [John Lardner, combat correspondent; Iwo Jima, 6 March 1945]

By their victory, the 3rd, 4th, and 5th Marine Divisions . . . have made an accounting to their country which only history will be able to value fully. Among the Americans who served on Iwo Jima, **uncommon valor was a common virtue**.
    [Fleet Adm. Chester W. Nimitz, USN (the last six words are inscribed on the Marine Corps War Memorial); 16 March 1945]

The Marine pilots were superb. They would fly down a gun barrel.
    [LtCmdr. Edgar Hoaglund, USN; Philippine Islands, March 1945]

Thank God for the Marines!
    [an Army Air Corps B-29 crewman, after his crippled bomber made an emergency landing on Iwo Jima, May 1945]

Thank God for the United States Marine Corps!
    [Eleanor Roosevelt (wife of Franklin D. Roosevelt, President of the United States), 1945]

What shall I say of the gallantry with which these Marines have fought? . . . I cannot write of their splendid gallantry without tears coming to my eyes.
    [MGen. James G. Harbord (1866-1947), USA; writing in *Leaves from a War Diary*]

The deadliest weapon in the world is a Marine and his rifle.
    [Gen. John J. "Black Jack" Pershing (1860-1948), USA]

The Marine Corps has been called by the *New York Times* the

"elite" Corps of this country. I think it is the "elite" of the world.
[Adm. William F. "Bull" Halsey, USN; 11 June 1949]

They [the Marines] have a propaganda machine that is almost equal
to Stalin's.
[Harry S. Truman, U.S. President (referring to Josef W. Stalin,
the Russian dictator); in a letter, 29 August 1950]

They are faced with impossible odds. But, these Marines have the
swagger, confidence, and hardness that must have been in
Stonewall Jackson's Army of the Shennandoah. I cling to the hope
of victory.
[British Liaison Officer, Korea, 15 September 1950]

The Marines and the Navy have never shone more brightly than
this morning.
[Gen. Douglas MacArthur, USA; Inchon, 15 September 1950]

I have just returned from visiting the Marines at the front, and
there is not a finer fighting organization in the world!
[Gen. Douglas MacArthur, USA; Korea, 21 September 1950]

It is my conviction that the successful assault on Inchon could have
been accomplished only by United States Marines.
[RAdm. James Doyle, USN; Korea, 1950]

The First Marine Division is the most efficient and courageous
combat unit I have ever seen or heard of.
[MGen. Frank E. Lowe, USA; Korea, 1950]

You cannot exaggerate about the Marines. They are convinced to
the point of arrogance that they are the most ferocious fighters on
Earth. And, the amusing thing about it is that they are.
[Kevin Keaney, USN chaplain; Korea, 1951]

Do not attack the First Marine Division. They fight like devils.
Leave the Marine yellowlegs alone. Strike the American Army.
[a captured Chinese Army Headquarters directive to Chinese
Army troops in Korea, 1951]

Panic sweeps my men when they face the American Marines.
[A captured North Korean major, Korea, 1951]

There is no better group of fighting men anywhere in the world than in the Marine Corps.
[Sen. Irving M. Ives, in the *Congressional Record*, April 1951]

Fortunately, God loves the Marines.
[Samuel E. Morrison, American naval historian; 1951]

The safest place in Korea was right behind a platoon of Marines. Lord, how they could fight!
[MGen. Frank E. Lowe, USA; Korea, 26 January 1952]

The more Marines I have around me, the better I like it. *[and also]* The American Marines have it [pride] and benefit from it. They are tough, cocky, sure of themselves and their buddies. They can fight and they know it.
[Gen. Mark W. Clark (1896-1984), USA]

The Marine Corps had an infinite capacity for demanding that which is required to be successful in combat. *[and also]* A warrior culture is absolutely necessary for success in combat. *[and also]* I am vehemently opposed to sending Marines on peace-keeping missions. I would prefer to leave all of that [expletive] to the Army. Hell, they don't want to fight anyway.
["Doc" Lane, USN corpsman assigned to B/1/4; late 1950s]

The Marines' best propaganda has usually been the naked event.
[Marc Parrott, *Hazard*, 1962]

A man who will go where his colors go, without asking; who will fight a phantom foe in jungle and mountain range, without counting; and who will suffer and die in the midst of incredible hardship, without complaint; is still what he has always been, from Imperial Rome to sceptered Britain to democratic America. He is the stuff of which legends are made . . . He has been called, United States Marine.
[LtCol. T.E. Fehrenbach, USA; *This Kind of War*, 1964]

The amphibious landing of U.S. Marines on September 15, 1950, at Inchon, on the west coast of Korea, was one of the most audacious and spectacularly successful amphibious landings in all naval history.
[Bernard Brodie, *A Guide to Naval Strategy*, 1965]

The appearance of [United States] Marines on foreign soil has always in the past indicated the beginning of extremely dangerous military adventures.
[Article in *Krasnaya* (Soviet Union *Red Star*), eight days after a U.S. Marine battalion (3/9) landed in Vietnam on 8 March 1965]

The eyes of the nation and the eyes of the entire world, the eyes of history itself, are on that brave little band of Marine defenders who hold the pass at Khe Sanh.
[Lyndon B. Johnson, U.S. President; during the 77 day siege of the U.S. Marine bastion at Khe Sanh, 19 February 1968]

Marines defending are like Antichrists at vespers.
[Michael Herr, *Dispatches*, 1968]

United States Marines treat their service as if it was some kind of cult. Like fanatics, they plaster their emblem on everything they own. They worship their Commandant as if he were a God. They make weird animal noises like a band of savages, and they'll fight like rabid dogs at the drop of a hat. Yet, their high spirits, camaraderie, and brotherhood astound me. They are the finest men I have had the pleasure to meet.
[William R. Durant, a Canadian; speaking in 1969]

It is friendship, and something beyond friendship, that binds the Marine Corps together.
[Donald T. Regan, U.S. Secretary of the Treasury; 1981]

Retrieving wounded comrades from the field of fire is a Marine Corps tradition more sacred than life.
[Robert Pisor, *The End of the Line*, 1982]

We have *two companies of Marines* running rampant all over the

northern half of this island, and *three Army regiments* pinned down in the southwest corner, doing nothing. What the hell is going on?
  [Gen. John W. Vessey Jr., USA, Chairman of the Joint Chiefs of Staff; during the assault on Grenada, October 1983]

Some people spend an entire lifetime wondering if they made a difference in the world. But, the Marines don't have that problem!
[and also] Today, the world looks to America for leadership. And, America looks to its Corps of Marines.
  [Ronald Reagan, U.S. President; 1985]

Lying offshore, ready to act, the presence of ships and Marines sometimes means much more than just having air power or ship's fire, when it comes to deterring a crisis. And the ships and Marines may not have to do anything but lie offshore. It is hard to lie offshore with a C-141 or C-130 full of airborne troops.
  [Gen. Colin Powell, USA; Chairman of the Joint Chiefs of Staff]

I cannot think of Iwo [Jima] without seeing again those dirty, exhausted, frightened, magnificent Marines who gave so unselfishly of themselves. The vision of their sacrifice is seared forever in my memory.
  [SSgt. Arvin S. Gibson, USA; *In Search of Angels*, 1990]

I can't say enough about the two Marine divisions. If I used words like *brilliant*, it would really be an under-description of the absolutely superb job they did in breaching the so-called impenetrable barrier. It was a classic -- absolutely classic -- military breaching of a very, very tough minefield, barbed wire, fire-trenches type barrier.
  [Gen. H. Norman Schwarzkopf, USA; speaking in Saudi Arabia after the battle for Kuwait, 27 February 1991]

They told [us] to open up the Embassy, or "we'll blow you away." And then they looked up and saw the Marines on the roof with these really big guns, and they said in Somali, "Igaralli ahow," which means "Excuse me, I didn't mean it, my mistake."
  [Karen Aguilar, in the U.S. Embassy; Mogadishu, Somalia, 1991]

The Marines will be needed as long as America needs defending.
  [J. Robert Moskin, American historian; 1992]

Take away the guns and uniforms, and it can sometimes be difficult to tell a Marine from a Jesuit. *[and also]* The Corps' ultimate weapon isn't the Hornet fighter or the Abrams tank. It's the young Marine with the M-16A2 rifle.
  [Hans Halberstadt, *U.S. Marine Corps*, 1993]

Marines know how to use their bayonets. Army bayonets may as well be paper-weights. *[and also]* The Marines invade, then go home. The Army has to do the occupying.
  [*Navy Times,* 7 November 1994]

Every Marine above the rank of Corporal can tell you what it takes to be a leader. It's spelled out clearly and drilled in relentlessly. And, it pays off under fire. *[and also]* Marines do more with less, and they like it that way. *[and also]* Navy chaplains [serving with the Marines]! You gotta' love a man of the cloth when the cloth is camouflage.
  [*Navy Times*, 7 November 1994]

Marines are warriors, a profession Americans have always looked upon with awe. *[and also]* The Marine Corps is a brotherhood. *[and also]* Marines divide the world into two classes: Marines, and those who aren't good enough to be Marines.
  [David B. Wood, *A Sense of Values*, 1994]

"First to fight" isn't just a motto, it's a way of life. From the day they were formed at Tun Tavern 221 years ago, Marines have distinguished themselves on battlefields around the world. From the fighting tops of the *Bonhomme Richard* to the sands of the Barbary Coast, from the swamps of New Orleans to the halls of Montezuma, from Belleau Wood to the Argonne Forest, to Guadalcanal and Iwo Jima, and Okinawa and Inchon, and Chosin Reservoir and Hue City, and Quang Tri and Dong Ha, and Beirut and Grenada and Panama, and Somalia and Bosnia and a thousand unnamed battlefields in Godforsaken corners of the globe. Marines have distinguished themselves by their bravery and stubbornness and aggressive spirit and sacrifice, and love of country and loyalty to one another. They've done it for you and me and this country we all love so dearly. They asked for nothing more than the honor of being a United States Marine.

  [RAdm. "Jay" R. Stark, USN, president of the Naval War College; 10 November 1995]

Marines I see as two breeds, Rottweilers or Dobermans, because Marines come in two varieties, big and mean, or skinny and mean. They're aggressive on the attack and tenacious on defense. They've got really short hair and they always go for the throat. *[and also]* I like the fact that Marines are stubborn. I like the way Marines obey orders. I like the way Marines make the most of the press. I like the wholehearted professionalism of the Marines.

  [RAdm. "Jay" R. Stark, USN, president of the Naval War College; 10 November 1995]

The United States Marine Corps, with its fiercely proud tradition of excellence in combat, its hallowed rituals, and its unbending code of honor, is part of the fabric of American myth. *[and also]* The Marines are rebels *with* a cause. *[and also]* The average Marine lance corporal speaks with more self confidence to a reporter than does the average Army captain.

  [Thomas E. Ricks, *Making The Corps*, 1997]

Always Faithful. It is the motto of the Marine Corps, but so much more than that. It's a code, a way of life, of serving one's country. Always Faithful, loyal above all else, to God, Country, and Corps. It is the common thread through Marines, young and old, past and present, that makes the Marine Corps more than a branch of the military; it's a brotherhood, a band of brothers.

  [Paul Keider, age 16; in his high school Speech Competition]

Apparently the Marine Corps has a training program that can knock out even a former heavyweight champion of the world.

  [Sgt. Kevin Robinson, USA; "Reddick bows out after 11 days of Marine boot camp," in *Army Link News,* 3 March 1997]

There is not another Marine alive who has not heard of The Great Santini. He never quit fighting, never surrendered, and never gave up. He died like a king. He died like The Great Santini.
[Pat Conroy (son of deceased Col. Donald "The Great Santini" Conroy, USMC), in the funeral eulogy for his father, May 1998]

In the Marines, everyone -- sergeant, mechanic, cannoneer, supply man, clerk, aviator, cook -- is a rifleman first. *[and also]* Marines get the job done *because* they are Marines. They make a virtue out of necessity. The men, not the gear, make the difference.
[Col. Daniel P. Bolger, USA; *Death Ground*, 1999]

I'd give a million dollars to be a Marine.
[Riddick Bowe, former heavyweight boxing champion of the world; who completed only 11 days of USMC boot camp at Parris Island before dropping out on 21 February 1997, quoted in *The Detroit News*, 16 April 2000]

The Marine Corps will continue to play a pivotal role in any crisis that threatens life's most treasured commodity, freedom.
[William Cohen, U.S. Secretary of Defense; September 2000]

The U.S. Marines are ready, responsive, and relevant. When you live at the tip of the spear, there is no room for second best.
[Bell Helicopter Public Affairs statement, September 2000]

They [the Marines in Vietnam] believed in each other. They knew the danger, but they also knew their responsibility and their code.
[Adrienne Busby, in her 12th grade term paper, 16 March 2001]

They are America's Warriors, and they are ready . . . These are United States Marines, and they are dangerous. They are poised, if and when the order comes, to wreak havoc on the enemies of their country.
[Phil McCombs, in the *Washington Post*, 13 September 2001]

I have respect for the Marines. God bless them, every one.
[Sgt. William Stuart, USAF; Afghanistan, 27 September 2002]

If I am going to die, I want to die like a Marine.
[Erik Reams, a 7-year-old second grade student; during medical treatment for a brain tumor (by order of the Commandant, Erik was made an "honorary Private" in the Corps), November 2002]

Semper Fidelis is not just another catchy Latin motto; it is a philosophical sword in the stone that sets Marines apart.
[Margaret Bone, in *The Yellow Sheet*, spring 2003]

The [expletive] Marines have killed every living thing except the snakes and the lizards!
[Capt. James A. Smith, USA; viewing the carnage after U.S. Marines battled through Nasiriyah, Iraq, 24 March 2003]

In this town it is hip to love America, it is cool to be a patriot, and ***it is special to be a U.S. Marine!***
[editorial, *Jacksonville Daily News* (Jacksonville, NC, home of MCB Camp Lejeune and MCAS New River), March 2003]

They were U.S. Marines and Devil Dogs. Not hyphenated Marines, just Marines, the Few and the Proud . . . They are truly a band of brothers.
[Richard Tompkins, UPI correspondent; writing *With the Marines in Iraq*, 21 April 2003]

Shoot at them and they will kill you. Marines *know* how to fight. Correction: Marines *like* to fight!
[F.J. Bing West, writing "Quagmire?" in *The Wall Street Journal*, 23 July 2003]

Fighting Words from U.S. Marines

Now it is the Marines' turn to speak up. When U.S. Marines talk about their Corps they speak of pride, loyalty, and honor. But most of all they speak about what they do best -- *fighting!*

Since the first Marine amphibious raid in March 1776, Marine Warriors have epitomized excellence in combat. Warrior Spirit! Commitment! First to Fight! A Few Good Men! All for one, one for all! In the Corps this is the stuff of legend, the qualities that exemplify the Warrior Culture of the U.S. Marines.

Below are fighting words from the world's warrior elite, the proud Brotherhood of Marines. You will find no mention of "politically correct" conduct, no sensitivity-session childishness. There are no administrative edicts from bean-counters. You will not read "in-the-rear-with-the-gear" procedures from REMF paper-pushers, no logistics theories. Nothing about social etiquette or silly gender compromises. There are no dry directives from staff pogues or library assistants.

Instead, you will hear Marine Warriors talking about their fighting Corps in action. Marines, here is your fighting heritage:

Gone to Florida to fight the Indians. Will be back when the war is over.
[Col. Archibald Henderson, USMC (CMC); in a note that he pinned to his office door, 1836]

I would rather command a *company* of Marines than a *brigade* of [U.S. Army] volunteers.
[Capt. John R.F. Tattnall, CSMC; explaining why he resigned his U.S. Army commission, as a colonel, to assume the rank of a captain in the Confederate States Marine Corps, November 1862]

Civilize 'em with a Krag.
  [credo of U.S. Marines in China in regard to their Model 1896
  Krag-Jorgensen rifles, during the Boxer Rebellion, 1900]

Retreat, Hell! We just got here!
  [Capt. Lloyd Williams, USMC; to the retreating French Army
  commander who pleaded with the Marines to flee from the
  attacking German Army in Belleau Wood, France, 2 June 1918]

Come on, you sons of bitches! Do you want to live forever?
  [GySgt. Daniel J. "Dan" Daly, USMC; near Lucy-'le-Bocage as
  he led the Fifth Marines' attack into Belleau Wood, 6 June 1918]

I have only two men out of my company and 20 out of some other
company. We need support, but it is almost suicide to try to get
it here as we are swept by machine gun fire and a constant barrage
is on us. I have no one on my left and only a few on my right.
I will hold.
  [1stLt. Clifton B. Cates, USMC; Belleau Wood, 19 July 1918]

The record of our Corps is one which will bear comparison with
that of the most famous military organizations in the world's
history.
  [Gen. John A. Lejeune, USMC (CMC); in the first Marine Corps
  Birthday Message to all U.S. Marines, 10 November 1921]

For the Marine Corps there is no peace.
  [Maj. Edwin N. Demby, USMC; years later while Secretary of
  the Navy (1921-1924)]

I've got some bad news, and some good news. The bad news is
that we will be filling sandbags until the next Japanese attack
comes. The good news is that we have plenty of sand.
  [unidentified gunnery sergeant, USMC; on Wake Island after the
  initial Japanese attacks, 11 December 1941]

God favors the bold and the strong of heart.
  [MGen. Alexander A. Vandegriff, USMC; to his Marines before
  D-Day at Guadalcanal, August 1942]

He contributed materially to the defeat and virtually the annihilation of a Japanese Regiment.
  [LtCol. Lewis B. "Chesty" Puller, USMC; recommending that Sgt. John "Manila John" Basilone be awarded the Medal of Honor for gallantry on Guadalcanal on 24 October 1942]

You'll never get a Purple Heart hiding in a foxhole! Follow me!
  [Capt. Henry P. Crowe, USMC; Guadalcanal, 13 January 1943]

If you want to fight, join the Marines!
  [Marine Corps Recruiting Poster, c World War II]

They [Women Marines] don't have a nickname, and they don't need one. They get their basic training in a Marine atmosphere, at a Marine post. They inherit the traditions of the Marines. They *are* Marines.
  [LtGen. Thomas Holcomb, USMC; *Concise History*, 1943]

The Marines have a way of making you afraid -- not of dying, but of not doing your job.
  [1stLt. Bonnie Little, USMC; Tarawa, 20 November 1943]

Casualties many, percentage of dead not known, combat efficiency: we are winning.
  [Col. David M. Shoup, USMC; Tarawa, 21 November 1943]

I can never again see a United States Marine without experiencing a feeling of reverence.
  [MGen. Julian C. Smith, USMC; in a letter to his wife after the horrible struggle for Tarawa, 1943]

My only answer as to why the Marines get the toughest jobs is because the average Leatherneck is a much better fighter.
  [2ndLt. Richard C. Kennard, USMC; Peleliu, September 1944]

I prefer to be lavish with ordnance but stingy with my men's lives.
  [Col. Bucky Harris, USMC; Peleliu, September 1944]

We're not accustomed to occupying defensive positions. It's

destructive to morale.
[LtGen. Holland "Howlin' Mad" Smith, USMC; Iwo Jima, 1945]

Victory was never in doubt. What was in doubt was whether there would be any of us left alive to dedicate our cemetery at the end, or whether the last Marine would die knocking out the last Japanese gunner.
[MGen. Graves Erskine, USMC; dedicating the Marine Corps cemetery on Iwo Jima after the bloody victory, March 1945]

The bended knee is not a tradition of our Corps.
[Gen. Alexander A. Vandegriff, USMC (CMC); to the Senate Naval Affairs Committee, 5 May 1946]

Hit quickly, hit hard, and keep on hitting.
[LtGen. Holland M. "Howlin' Mad" Smith, USMC; *Coral and Brass*, 1949]

Don't forget that you're First Marines! Not all the communists in Hell can overrun you!
[Col. Lewis B. "Chesty" Puller, USMC; rallying his First Marine Regiment near Chosin Reservoir, Korea, December 1950]

If they start to pull back from that line, even one foot, I want you to open fire on them. **We're here to fight!**
[Col. Lewis B. "Chesty" Puller, USMC; in a radio call to his artillery officer at Koto-ri, Korea, after an Army captain had asked about his line of retreat, December 1950]

Those poor bastards. They've got us surrounded. Now we can fire in any direction. They won't get away this time. *[and later]* They have us right where we want them. *[and still later]* That simplifies our problem of getting to these people and killing them.
[Col. Lewis B. "Chesty" Puller, USMC; visiting the wounded in the regimental hospital tent, when told that his First Marine Regiment was surrounded by seven Chinese Divisions near the Chosin Reservoir, Korea, December 1950]

Remember, whatever you write, this was no retreat. All that

happened was that we found more Chinese behind us than in front of us, so we about-faced and attacked.
[Col. Lewis B. "Chesty" Puller, USMC; to the media after the breakout from Chosin Reservoir, Korea, December 1950]

We're not retreating. We're just attacking in another direction.
[MGen. Oliver P. Smith, USMC; Korea, December 1950]

Only 14 more shooting days until Christmas.
[hand-painted words, photographed on a Marine tank during the breakout from Chosin Reservoir, Korea, 11 December 1950]

Success in battle. In my opinion that is the only objective of military training.
[LtGen. Lewis B. "Chesty" Puller, USMC; in his courtroom testimony at MCRD Parris Island, 2 August 1956]

The Marine Corps is the best place to learn the art of war. *[and also]* Paper work will ruin any military force. *[and also]* You don't hurt 'em if you don't hit 'em.
[LtGen. Lewis B. "Chesty" Puller, USMC; in *Marine*, 1962]

Over the years the Marines built up a deserved reputation for bravery, devotion to duty, and never striking their colors.
[LtCol. Paul H. Douglas (1892-1976) USMC; speaking years after his military service while a member of the U.S. Senate]

Get the blade into the enemy. This is the main principle in bayonet fighting. It is the blade that kills.
[Marine Corps Association, *Guidebook for Marines*, 1962]

Being ready is not what matters. What matters is winning after you get there.
[LtGen. Victor H. "Brute" Krulak, USMC; to his Marines headed for Vietnam, April 1965]

But the thing I'm most proud of is that I was a Marine Corps fighter pilot. I am a U.S. Marine, and I'll be one 'till I die!
[Capt. Theodore "Ted" Williams, USMC; universally considered

the best hitter ever to play major league baseball, and the last major league player with a season batting average of .400 or more (.406 with the Boston Red Sox in 1941), the day of his induction into the Baseball Hall of Fame, 25 July 1966]

They hit us all of a sudden. I saw this one guy yelling and waving his arms around. He looked like a squad leader or platoon commander. I shot him. We were shooting them with pistols and throwing grenades like they were going out of style.
[PFC Robert Calloway, USMC; in *Pacific Stars and Stripes*, describing a firefight in Vietnam on 8 August 1966]

.30 cal's won't hurt you if your mind's right.
[handwritten sign, posted in the Marine Corps helicopter pilot's ready-room tent at Phu Bai, Vietnam, 1967]

Those young Marines! God, they were magnificent!
[Maj. Matthew P. Caulfield, USMC; in *Marine Corps Gazette*, referring to Marines in "Leatherneck Square," Vietnam, in 1967]

Helicopters! And, the valor and skill of the pilots has outrun the book. The stars on their Air Medals are matched only by the stars in their crowns.
[LtGen. Victor H. "Brute" Krulak, USMC; writing about Marine Corps helicopter crews in Vietnam, 11 July 1967]

You Marines at Khe Sanh will be remembered in the American history books!
[Col. David E. Lownds, USMC; Khe Sanh, January 1968]

When a Marine in Vietnam is wounded, surrounded, low on ammunition or water, he looks to the sky. He knows the choppers are coming.
[Gen. Leonard F. Chapman Jr. (1913-2000), USMC (CMC)]

It seemed as though the pilots were trying to twist the fuselage around to escape the rounds. From the ground we could see the tracers converge on the tailpipes. Yet the pilots came around again and again as though it was a training flight. The war seemed to

stop. All eyes were fixed on the planes. I don't know what the others felt, but my eyes were glued on the letters M-A-R-I-N-E-S painted on the fuselages.
[Maj. Matthew P. Caulfield, USMC; writing "India Six" about combat in Vietnam, in *Marine Corps Gazette*, July 1969]

A special fraternity exists between those who have met and survived the challenges of combat.
[Col. James E. Johnson (1919-2000), USMC]

It's what you wear on your collar -- the Eagle, Globe, and Anchor -- that puts you in the Brotherhood of Marines.
[BGen. Carl E. Mundy Jr., USMC; 10 November 1984]

Marines die. That's what we're here for. But the Marine Corps lives forever. And that means *YOU* will live forever.
[the mythical GySgt. Hartman, USMC; portrayed by real-life GySgt. R. Lee Ermey, USMC; a U.S. Marine Drill Instructor using his own choice of words in *Full Metal Jacket*, 1987]

We're warriors, and people who support warriors, and we must always keep that focus.
[Gen. Alfred M. Gray Jr., USMC (CMC); on the day he became Commandant of the Marine Corps in 1987]

To be a Marine pilot is to be the chosen of the chosen.
[Capt. Jon Boulle, USMC; in *Life on the Line*, 1988]

The Marines have sustained themselves as the finest fighting organization this country has ever produced.
[Capt. James H. Webb Jr., USMC; later an author, lecturer, entrepreneur, and Secretary of the Navy (1987-1989)]

We carry on our shoulders a proud tradition that has been molded by hundreds of thousands who have gone before us . . . If I got shot, a Marine would never leave me on the battlefield.
[Col. Barney Barnum, USMC; in *Valor*, 1989]

I have never seen so many [Marines] ready to kick somebody's

[expletive]. We wanted to fight!
  [Cpl. David J. Gomez, USMC; in *Operation Buffalo*, 1991]

We will succeed in our mission because we are well trained and well equipped, and because we are U.S. Marines.
  [LtGen. Walter Boomer, USMC; Saudi Arabia, February 1991]

A Marine's most sought after privilege is to be able to fight for another Marine.
  [MGen. Mike Myatt, USMC; Kuwait, 1991]

I hope the Iraqis are good lovers, because they sure can't fight.
  [LCpl. William Washington, USMC; 27 February 1991]

Every Marine is, first and foremost, a rifleman. All other conditions are secondary.
  [Gen. Alfred M. Gray Jr., USMC (CMC 1987-1991)]

The American Marine will march down the barrel of an enemy rifle for you. It continually has amazed me over the years just how good the individual Marine can be.
  [Capt. Paul Goodwin, USMC; *No Shining Armor*, 1992]

[Your essay] is a pitiful attempt to boost your ego by comparing yourself to better men [Marines] flying better aircraft. Your F-16 should have a blue stripe painted around the nose and "For Training Use Only" stenciled on the fuselage.
  [unidentified lieutenant colonel, USMC; responding to a U.S. Air Force essay in *Aimpoint: Naval Strike Warfare Review*, 1993]

In 32 years of service and combat in three wars, I have never met or known finer Marines or better Americans than those who served in Vietnam.
  [Col. McDonald D. "Mac" Tweed, USMC; in a letter, quoted in *Pop-A-Smoke*, August 1993]

The pride and discipline of a Marine is unmatched and always will be. Semper Fi!
  [unidentified lance corporal, USMC; in *A Sense of Values*, 1994]

I love my Corps and my country. I shall continue to do my job to the best of my ability. Why do I stay with it? Honor, duty, commitment, loyalty, love of God, Country, Corps.
[unidentified sergeant, USMC; in *A Sense of Values*, 1994]

Civilians cannot understand us because they are not one of us. The Corps -- we love it, live it, and will die for it. If you have never been in it you shall never understand it. Semper Fidelis!
[unidentified lance corporal, USMC; in *A Sense of Values*, 1994]

We all know our job and we're honest and I trust Marines with my life and they trust me with theirs. That's something civilians don't understand.
[unidentified PFC, USMC; in *A Sense of Values*, 1994]

The lifeblood of our Corps is the individual Marine.
[Marine Corps Recruiting Poster, c 1990s]

I love the Corps for those intangible possessions that cannot be issued: pride, honor, integrity, and being able to carry on the traditions for generations of warriors past.
[Cpl. Jeff Sornig, USMC; in *Navy Times*, 7 November 1994]

This old Grunt thanks you for the magnificent, heroic, and often fatal risks you took for your fellow Marines. God bless you and keep you safe. There is *nothing* like Marine Air! Semper Fi!
[Mick Carey, Marine veteran; in *Pop-A-Smoke*, 1 May 1995]

We fought for each other, or to uphold the honor of the Corps. That was what mattered.
[Capt. Angus Deming, USMC; in *Newsweek*, 7 August 1995]

You know that you will never be abandoned. Your Marine brothers may fail in their effort to save you, and they may even lose their own lives, but they *must* try. They have no choice. *[and also]* We might succeed, or we might fail, but we would succeed or fail together. There was no other Marine Corps way.
[Capt. Marion F. Sturkey, USMC; *Bonnie-Sue*, 1996]

There is a fellowship of valor that links all U.S. Marines, past, present, and future.
  [Col. Joseph H. Alexander, USMC; *A Fellowship of Valor*, 1997]

Every Marine has been trained as a rifleman, for it is the rifleman who must close with and destroy the enemy. *[and also]* A vigorous bayonet assault, executed by Marines eager to drive home cold steel, can strike terror into the ranks of the enemy. *[and also]* The purpose of offensive combat is to destroy the enemy and his will to fight.
  [Marine Corps Association, *Guidebook for Marines*, 1997]

General Hyakutake [Imperial Japanese Army] began to curse the day he had ever encountered the United States Marines.
  [Col. Joseph H. Alexander, USMC; *A Fellowship of Valor*, 1997]

For over 221 years our Corps has done two things for this great Nation. We make Marines, and we win battles.
  [Gen. Charles C. Krulak, USMC (CMC); 5 May 1997]

The Corps made me a better man, improved me in every way. It gave me pride and self-respect that can never be taken away.
  [John G. Snell, Marine veteran; in *Leatherneck*, November 1997]

Being a Marine comes from the eagle, globe, and anchor that is tattooed on the soul of everyone who wears the Marine uniform.
  [LtCol. Jeffrey Wilkinson, USMC; in *Marine Corps Gazette*, December 1997]

Marines lay claim to distinction as America's premier expeditionary force. *[and also]* Marines enjoy a reputation for prowess in combat. *[and also]* Being a Marine has been likened to a calling -- an almost religious commitment to the Corps.
  [Gen. Carl E. Mundy Jr., USMC; in *The Marines*, 1998]

It is the individual Marine -- not machines or technology -- that defines our success in war. *[and also]* Our focus rests, as it always has, upon the enhancement of the individual Marine, and his ability to win in combat. *[and also]* These Marines will be forged in the

same furnace of shared hardship and tough training that has produced the world's finest warriors for generations.
[Gen. Charles C. Krulak, USMC (CMC); in *The Marines*, 1998]

It was the Marines who won at Belleau Wood, the Marines who won at Guadalcanal, the Marines who led the way at Inchon. And that is exactly the way the Corps' heroes -- big and small -- would have it, for the Corps is less of the flesh than of the spirit.
[LtGen. Victor H. "Brute" Krulak, USMC; in *The Marines*, 1998]

The central fact of life in the Corps is still that the Marine Rifleman is the key to winning battles.
[Col. John G. Miller, USMC; in *The Marines*, 1998]

Marine Air is a superb combined arms weapon, and today's Flying Leathernecks command a world-wide reputation for skill and 'elan that is second to none.
[LtCol. Ronald J. Brown, USMC; in *The Marines*, 1998]

Believe in your training. Believe in your equipment. Believe in your leaders. But, most of all, believe in yourself. It will carry you through and make you a champion.
[Col. James E. Johnson, USMC; 1919-2000]

What we were doing was not a job, not even a profession, but a calling. For me, joining the Marines was the closest thing to becoming a priest.
[Gen. Anthony C. Zinni, USMC; March 2000]

All who now wear, or have ever worn, the eagle, globe, and anchor share a common bond.
[Charles Robb, Marine veteran; writing years later while a U.S. Senator, September 2000]

The patriotic service and valor of our aviation units, past and present, is a legacy of our Corps.
[SgtMaj. A.L. McMichael, USMC (Sergeant Major of the Marine Corps); in a letter, September 2000]

We are United States Marines, and for two and a quarter centuries we have defined the standards of courage, esprit, and military prowess.
    [Gen. James L. Jones Jr., USMC (CMC); 10 November 2000]

I was a Marine Corps aviator doing what I was trained to do and getting to work with my fellow Marines in combat. They were the best of the best. *[and also]* Those who have never experienced the camaraderie that exists between Marines who have fought together in combat and almost died, well, they haven't lived.
    [Capt. Roger A. Herman, USMC; writing "A Very Special Club" in *The Log Book*, summer 2001]

Saying, "It gives great honor to our brother Ira," they went through a prayer ritual that was so beautiful, so moving and poignant, that we stood there transfixed, speechless . . . It is the Corps that produced such men as Ira Hayes, and these two lonely warriors who came all the way from Arizona just to pay homage to a fallen brother. God bless these wonderful Marines!
    [Col. John W. Ripley, USMC; writing about two elderly Pima Indians at the grave of PFC Ira Hayes, USMC (one of the Iwo Jima flag-raisers); in Arlington National Cemetery, 4 July 2001]

When you are in the military and at war, there is no such thing as innocence. It's called kill or be killed.
    [MGen. J.J. Johnson, USMC; 19 July 2001]

They should be caught, drawn and quartered, decapitated, and their ugly [expletive] heads put on pikes in front of the White House.
    [Maj. Bill F. Weaver, USMC; 12 September 2001]

It is time to kick [expletive]! Whatever it takes!
    [2ndLt. John E. Fales, USMC; 12 September, 2001]

I'll take any job they want to give me . . . I'm prepared to [reenlist] as an E-1. I can still shoot expert and pass the PT test.
    [Capt. Allyn J. Hinton, USMC; 12 September 2001]

I don't care what God they believe in but they better get [expletive]

close to him, 'cause they are about to meet him face to face.
[Sgt. Robert J. "Bob" Kowalk, USMC; 13 September 2001]

Let the enemy know the full fury of an America that has been
wronged and demands retribution. Kill them all! Semper Fi!
[Sgt. Arthur W. Larsen, USMC; 13 September 2001]

Marines are built through the ethos of struggle and sacrifice.
[Gen. James L. Jones Jr., USMC (CMC 1999-2003); in a letter
of condolence to the 13 year old son of a deceased Marine]

Those four men [the helicopter crew] climbed into those great big
green monsters [USMC helicopters]; they put everything on the line
to help those poor miserable Grunts out there in the bush, almost
always laying their lives on the line. They were the bravest, most
selfless, most inspiring men I have ever known in my life. I loved
each and every one of them for their courage.
[GySgt. Larry Powell, USMC; writing about Marine Corps
helicopter crews in Vietnam, years later, on 21 September 2001]

Marines everywhere can take pride in their contributions to our
great nation. We are a Corps born of an act of Congress,
consecrated in sacrifice, steeped in tradition, and tested in battle.
[Gen. James L. Jones Jr., USMC (CMC); 10 November 2001]

Every Marine is a rifleman first and foremost, a Marine first, last,
and always. *[and also]* You join the Marines to go to war.
[GySgt. Daniel E. Sims, USMC; in *Leatherneck*, February 2003]

The strength of our Corps will continue to be the resourcefulness
of the individual Marine.
[Gen. Michael W. Hagee, USMC (CMC); March 2003]

Together we will cross the Line of Departure, close with those
forces that choose to fight, and destroy them.
[MGen. James N. Mattis, USMC; in Kuwait, March 2003]

We're Marines! We took Iwo Jima! Baghdad ain't [expletive]!
[LCpl. John Rogers, USMC; as the Marines prepared to attack

across the Diyala Bridge into Baghdad, Iraq, 7 April, 2003]

My Marines showed no mercy. Outstanding!
[unidentified squad leader, USMC; speaking in Baghdad, Iraq, on 8 April 2003, quoted in the *New York Times Magazine*]

We have to get back to our unit. There is still fighting going on. We can't miss that!
[Cpl. Christopher Castro, USMC; speaking to the news media after he helped rescue seven Army POWs in Iraq, 13 April 2003]

Live or die, the most important thing to a Marine is accomplishing the mission.
[LtCol. David W. Szelowski, USMC; 19 May 2003]

I wish to thank the Marine Corps for bringing out the best in me.
[Olga P. Rogers, Marine veteran; in a letter on her 80th birthday, in *Leatherneck*, June 2003]

Marines went farther and faster than ever before. You've written new pages of history. Everyone who wears the eagle, globe, and anchor is proud of what you've done.
[Gen. Michael W. Hagee, USMC (CMC); Iraq, 17 June 2003]

Although I am soon to be 78 years old, I still consider myself to be a proud jarhead.
[Alva R. Perry, Marine veteran; in *Leatherneck*, June 2003]

. . . and for the history books . . . .

Two U.S. Marines, MGen. Smedley D. Butler and GySgt. Daniel J. "Dan" Daly, have *twice* been awarded the Medal of Honor:
MGen. Smedley D. Butler:
  1. Vera Cruz, Mexico, as a Major in 1914
  2. Ft. Reviere, Haiti, as a Major in 1915
GySgt. Daniel J. "Dan" Daly:
  1. Peking, China, as a Private in 1900
  2. Ft. Dipitie, Haiti, as a Gunnery Sergeant in 1915

Combat Axioms for Warriors

The Profession of Arms! Since time immemorial the professional warrior has always been a key player on the world stage.

Non-combatants look at warriors and see either honor and glory, or horror and hardship. Yet, down through the centuries the individual warrior has not concerned himself with what non-combatants see or believe. Instead, the warrior has only three immediate concerns: (1) loyalty to brothers-in-arms, (2) allegiance to cause, and (3) success in battle -- often called *staying alive* in battle. A true professional warrior possesses all three of these concerns. One or two will not suffice.

Success in battle, like success in any other human endeavor, hinges on proven principles. These principles do not change. Weapons change. Technology changes. Nations rise, nations fall. Causes come, causes go. Yet, the basic principles, or axioms, of warfare remain constant.

Below are many timeless Combat Axioms for Warriors (axioms attributed to U.S. Marines were listed in the previous chapter). Down through the ages, most of these axioms have come from men who have tasted the sting of battle. Professional warriors of today: read them, heed them, and *stay alive* in combat:

Our business in the field of fight
Is not to question, but to fight.
   [Homer, *The Iliad*, c 800 BC]

All warfare is based on deception. *[and also]* Do not thwart an enemy returning home. *[and also]* Invincibility lies in the defense; the possibility of victory in the attack. One defends when his strength is inadequate; he attacks when it is abundant.
   [Sun Tzu, *The Art of War*, c 500 BC]

Great deeds are usually wrought at great risk.
   [Herodotus (c 490-425 BC), Greek historian]

Danger gleams like sunshine to a brave man's eyes. *[and also]*
There is nothing like the sight of an enemy down on his luck.
  [Euripides (c 485-406 BC), Greek poet and playwright]

The bravest are surely those who have the clearest vision of what
is before them, glory and danger alike, and yet notwithstanding, go
out to meet it.
  [Thucydides (460-400 BC), Greek historian]

The Spartans do not ask how many the enemy number, but where
they are.
  [Ages of Sparta, venerated Spartan sage; c 415 BC]

In war, opportunity waits for no man.
  [Pericles, Athenian statesman; *The Peloponnesian War,* 404 BC]

Stand firm, for well you know that hardship and danger are the
price of glory!
  [Alexander the Great (356-323 BC), Greek conqueror; in India]

The greater the difficulty, the greater the glory.
  [Cicero (c 106-43 BC), Roman Consul and orator]

I came. I saw. I conquered.
  [Julius Caesar, Roman General; the entire text of his dispatch to
  the Roman Senate after his victory at the Battle of Zela, 47 BC]

Let them hate us as long as they fear us.
  [Caligula (c 12-41 AD), Roman Emperor]

The body of a dead enemy always smells sweet.
  [Aulus Vitellius, Roman Emperor; at Beariacum, 69 AD]

Let him who desires peace prepare for war.
  [Vegetius, Roman military strategist; c 400 AD]

The greatest happiness is to vanquish your enemies.
  [Genghis Khan (1162-1227), Mongol conqueror]

The infantry must ever be regarded as the very foundation and nerve of an army.
  [Niccolo Machiavelli, *Discourses*, 1517]

It is fighting at a great disadvantage to fight those who have nothing to lose.
  [Francesco Guiciardini, *Storia d'Italia*, 1564]

Cowards die many times before their deaths;
The valiant never taste of death but once.
  [William Shakespeare (1564-1616), *Julius Caesar*]

We few, we happy few, we band of brothers;
For he today that sheds his blood with me
Shall be my brother.
  [William Shakespeare (1564-1616), *Henry V*]

A man-o-war is the best ambassador.
  [Oliver Cromwell (1599-1658), Lord Protector of Ireland]

Battles are won by superiority of fire. *[and also]* He who tries to defend everything defends nothing.
  [Frederick the Great, King of Prussia; *Military Testament*, 1752]

The first blow is half the battle.
  [Oliver Goldsmith, British novelist; *She Stoops to Conquer*, 1773]

The battle, sir, is not to the strong alone. It is to the vigilant, the active, the brave!
  [Patrick Henry, American statesman; addressing the Virginia Convention of Delegates, 23 March 1775]

We must all hang together, or, we shall all hang separately.
  [Benjamin Franklin, American statesman; speaking immediately after signing the *Declaration of Independence*, 4 July 1776]

Let us beware of being lulled into a dangerous security of being weakened by internal contentions and diversions; of neglect in military exercises and disciplines in providing stores and arms and

munitions of war.
[Benjamin Franklin, American statesman; in a letter, 1784]

If we desire to avoid insult, we must be able to repel it. If we desire peace, it must be known that we are ready for war.
[Gen. George Washington, Continental Army; to The Congress while serving as U.S. President, 3 December 1793]

March to the sound of the guns.
[Duke of York, British noble; 1793]

No military leader has ever become great without audacity.
[MGen. Carl von Clausewitz, strategist; *Principles of War*, 1812]

Don't give up the ship! Fight her until she sinks!
[Capt. James Lawrence, USN; mortally wounded aboard his frigate, *USS Chesapeake*, 1 June 1813]

One man with courage is a majority.
[Thomas Jefferson (1743-1826), U.S. President]

Glory may be fleeting, but obscurity is forever. *[and also]* Moral forces, rather than numbers, decide victory. *[and also]* Good infantry is, without doubt, the sinew of an army. *[and also]* The bayonet has always been the weapon of the brave and the chief tool of victory. *[and also]* Four hostile newspapers are more to be feared than a thousand bayonets. *[and also]* Never interrupt your enemy when he is making a mistake.
[Napoleon Bonaparte, Emperor of France, charismatic military leader, and tactician; *Maxims of War*, 1831]

The best strategy is always to be strong. *[and also]* Blood is the price of victory.
[MGen. Carl von Clausewitz, strategist; *On War*, 1832]

Our flag still waves proudly from the walls . . . I shall never surrender nor retreat . . . I am determined to sustain myself as long as possible and die like a soldier who never forgets what is due to

his own honor and that of his country. Victory or Death!
  [LtCol. William B. Travis, Texas Volunteer Militia; in his last
  dispatch from the Alamo, 24 February 1836]

A great country cannot wage a little war.
  [Duke of Wellington, in the House of Lords, 16 January 1838]

We should forgive our enemies -- but *only* after they have been
hanged first.
  [Heinrich Heine (1797-1856), German philosopher]

I was too weak to defend, so I attacked. *[and also]* Do your duty
in all things. You can not do more. You should never do less.
  [Gen. Robert E. Lee (1807-1870), CSA]

There is a true glory and a true honor -- the glory of duty done, the
honor of the integrity of principle.
  [Gen. Robert E. Lee, CSA; in *Southern Historical Society Papers*]

In any fight, it's the first blow that counts the most. *[and also]*
War is fighting, and fighting means killing. *[and also]* Get 'em
skeered, and keep the skeer on 'em. *[and also]* I always make it a
rule to get there first'est with the most'est.
  [LtGen. Nathan Bedford Forrest (1821-1877), CSA]

I make no terms. I accept no compromises.
  [Jefferson Davis (1808-1889), C.S.A. President]

There! There! There is Jackson! Standing like a stone wall!
  [the rallying shout of an unidentified CSA officer at the first
  battle of Bull Run (also called, First Manassas), referring to
  BGen. Thomas J. "Stonewall" Jackson, CSA; 21 July 1861]

Why does Colonel Grigsby refer to me to learn how to deal with
mutineers? He should shoot them where they stand!
  [LtGen. Thomas J. "Stonewall" Jackson, CSA; May 1862]

Always mystify, mislead, and surprise the enemy. *[and also]* Duty
is ours, consequences are God's. *[and also]* What is life without

honor? Degradation is worse than death! *[and also]* An enemy routed, if hotly pursued, becomes panic-stricken and can be destroyed by half their number. *[and also]* To move swiftly, strike vigorously, and secure the fruits of victory is the secret of successful war. *[and also]* The business of the soldier is to fight, to find the enemy and strike him, invade his country, and do him all possible damage in the shortest possible time.
  [LtGen. Thomas J. "Stonewall" Jackson (1824-1863), CSA]

Success and glory are in the advance. Disaster and shame lurk in the rear.
  [MGen. John Pope, USA; in a General Order, 14 July 1862]

Charge the enemy, and remember old Virginia!
  [MGen. George E. Pickett, CSA; as he ordered the charge up Cemetery Ridge at Gettysburg, 3 July 1863]

We will fight them until Hell freezes over, and then we will fight them on the ice.
  [unidentified Confederate Army soldier; Gettysburg, 3 July 1863]

We must substitute *esprit* for numbers.
  [MGen. J.E.B. "Jeb" Stuart (1833-1864), CSA]

Get your enemy at a disadvantage and never, on any account, fight him on equal terms.
  [George Bernard Shaw, British author; *Arms and the Man*, 1894]

Courage is resistance to fear, mastery of fear, not absence of fear.
  [Samuel L. Clemens (1835-1910), a.k.a. Mark Twain]

My religious belief teaches me to feel as safe in battle as in bed.
  [LtGen. Thomas J. "Stonewall" Jackson, CSA; quoted years later, posthumously, in *Stonewall Jackson*, 1898]

Speak softly, and carry a big stick.
  [Col. Theodore "Teddy" Roosevelt, USA; U.S. Vice President, 2 September 1901]

I want no prisoners. I wish you to burn and kill. The more you burn and kill, the better it will please me.
  [BGen. Jacob H. Smith, USA; in his order to Maj. L.W.T. Waller, USA; in Samar, October 1901]

A man who is good enough to shed his blood for his Country is good enough to be given a square deal afterwards.
  [Col. Theodore "Teddy" Roosevelt, USA; U.S. President, 1903]

Those who cannot remember the past are condemned to repeat it.
  [George Santayana, *A Life of Reason*, 1906]

It is not the critic who counts . . . The credit belongs to the man who is actually in the arena, the man whose face is marred by dust and sweat and blood, the man who strives valiantly, the man who errs and comes up short again and again. The credit belongs to the man who knows the great enthusiasms, the great devotions, and spends himself in a worthy cause. The credit belongs to the man who -- at the best -- knows in the end the triumphs of high achievement. The credit belongs to the man who -- at the worst -- if he fails, at least fails while *Daring Greatly*. His place shall never be with those cold and timid souls who know neither defeat nor victory.
  [Col. Theodore "Teddy" Roosevelt, USA; former U.S. President, 23 April 1910]

The essence of war is violence. Moderation in war is imbecility.
  [Adm. Sir John Fisher, RN; in a letter, 25 April 1912]

Find the enemy and shoot him down. Anything else is nonsense. *[and also]* The aggressive spirit, the offensive, is the chief thing everywhere in war, and the air is no exception.
  [Baron Capt. Manfred von Richthofen, German Flying Service ("The Red Baron" of Germany); 80 air-to-air kills, WW I); 1917]

Aerial gunnery is 90 percent instinct and 10 percent aim.
  [Capt. Frederick C. Libby, British Royal Flying Corps (he was later in the U.S. Army Air Corps); 24 air-to-air kills, WW I]

A pacifist is as surely a traitor to his country and to humanity as is the most brutal wrongdoer.
  [Col. Theodore "Teddy" Roosevelt, USA; former U.S. President, 27 July 1917]

The will to conquer is the first condition of victory.
  [Marsh. Ferdinand Foch, French Army; *Principles of War*, 1920]

War hath no fury like a noncombatant.
  [Charles E. Montague, *Disenchantment*, 1922]

To be vanquished and yet not surrender, that is victory.
  [Marsh. Josef Pilsudski (1867-1935), Polish Army]

The advantage of sea power used offensively is that, when a fleet sails, one can never be sure where it is going to strike.
  [Sir Winston Churchill, *Their Finest Hour*, 1924]

People sleep peaceably in their beds at night only because rough men stand ready to do violence on their behalf.
  [Eric Blair (1903-1950), a.k.a. George Orwell, British novelist]

Through mobility we conquer.
  [motto of The Cavalry School, USA; Fort Riley, c 1930]

Appeasers believe that if you keep on throwing steaks to a tiger, the tiger will become a vegetarian.
  [Heywood H. Broun (1888-1939), American journalist]

Everyone will now be mobilized and all boys old enough to carry a spear will be sent to Addis Ababa. Married men will take their wives to carry food and cook. Those without wives will take any woman without a husband. Women with small babies need not go. The blind, those who cannot walk or for any reason cannot carry a spear are exempted. Anyone found at home after the receipt of this order will be hung.
  [Ethiopian Draft Notice, 1935]

To wound all ten fingers of a man is not so effective as to chop

one of them off. To rout ten of the enemy's divisions is not so effective as to annihilate one of them.
[Mao Tse-tung, Chairman of the People's Republic of China and Commander-in-Chief of the Army; December 1936]

Power emanates from the barrel of a gun.
[Mao Tse-tung, Chairman of the People's Republic of China and Commander-in-Chief of the Army; *On Guerrilla War*, 1938]

The more we sweat in peace, the less we bleed in war.
[Vijaya L. Pandit (1900-1990), Indian diplomat]

Victory at all costs, victory in spite of all terror, victory however long and hard the road may be; for without victory there is no survival.
[Sir Winston Churchill, British Prime Minister; speaking in the House of Commons, 13 May 1940]

We shall fight on the beaches. We shall fight in the landing grounds. We shall fight in the fields and in the streets. We shall fight in the hills. We shall never surrender.
[Sir Winston Churchill, British Prime Minister; speaking in the House of Commons, after the retreat from Dunkirk, 4 June 1940]

We are so outnumbered there's only one thing to do -- attack!
[Sir Andrew Cunningham, RN; at Taranto, 11 November 1940]

Sure I am of this. You have to endure to conquer. *[and also]* The only thing you must really do is never, never, never, give up. *[and also]* Nothing is worse than war? Dishonor is worse than war. Slavery is worse than war. *[and also]* Battles are won by slaughter and manoeuver.
[Sir Winston Churchill (1874-1965), Prime Minister of Britain]

Praise the Lord, and pass the ammunition!
[Lt. Howell M. Forgy, USN chaplain; to the Navy antiaircraft gun crews aboard the *USS New Orleans* during the Japanese air attack at Pearl Harbor, 7 December 1941]

Put your heart and soul into being an expert killer. The only good enemy is a dead enemy.
[Gen. George S. Patton Jr., USA (who was perhaps paraphrasing Gen. Philip H. Sheridan, USA; who stated c 1868, "The only good Indian is a dead Indian."); March 1942]

A pint of sweat will save a gallon of blood.
[Gen. George S. Patton Jr., USA; 8 November 1942]

If you don't like to fight, I don't want you around. You'd better get out before I kick you out.
[Gen. George S. Patton Jr., USA; to his staff, 24 March 1944]

Nobody ever won a war by dying for his country. You win a war by making the *other* poor dumb bastard die for *his* country. *[and also]* We don't want yellow cowards in this Army. They should be killed off like rats. If not, they will go home after this war is over and breed more cowards. Kill off the [expletive] cowards and we will have a nation of brave men . . . War is a bloody, killing business. You've got to spill their blood, or they will spill yours. Rip them up the belly! Shoot them in the guts!
[Gen. George S. Patton Jr., USA; addressing the soldiers of his Third Army, in England, 5 June 1944]

Lead me, follow me, or get out of my way!
[Gen. George S. Patton Jr. (1885-1945), USA]

Wars may be fought with weapons, but they are won by men.
[Gen. George S. Patton Jr., USA; in *The Cavalry Journal*]

Darkness is a friend to the skilled infantryman. *[and also]* In war the chief incalculable is the human will.
[Sir B.H. Liddell Hart, British Army; *Thoughts on War*, 1944]

See, Decide, Attack, Reverse.
[Col. Erich Hartmann, Luftwaffe; 352 air-to-air kills, WW II]

No sane man is unafraid in battle. But discipline produces in him a form of vicarious courage. *[and also]* To halt under fire is *folly*.

To halt under fire, and not fire back, is *suicide*.
[Gen. George S. Patton Jr., USA; quoted posthumously in *War as I Knew It*, 1947]

Answer violence with violence!
[Evita Peron (1919-1952), wife of the President of Argentina]

In war there is no second prize for the runner-up.
[Gen. Omar Bradley, USA; in *Military Review*, February 1950]

Give me an order to do it. I can break up Russia's five A-bomb nests in a week. And when I go up to meet Christ, I think I could explain to Him that I had saved civilization.
[MGen. Orvil A. Anderson, USAF; 1950]

It is fatal to enter any war without the will to win it.
[Gen. Douglas MacArthur, USA; 7 July 1952]

War is never prevented by running away from it.
[Air Marsh. Sir John Slessor, RAF; *Strategy for the West*, 1954]

Diplomacy has rarely been able to gain at the conference table what cannot be gained or held on the battlefield.
[Gen. Walter B. Smith, USA; on his return from the Geneva Conference on Korea and Indochina, 1954]

Diplomacy is the art of saying "Nice doggie" until you can find a bigger rock.
[Wynn Catlin, Texas political observer]

It is essential to understand that battles are won primarily in the hearts of men.
[Viscount Field Marsh. Montgomery, British Army; *The Memoirs of Field Marshall Montgomery*, 1958]

It isn't the size of the dog in the fight that counts. It's the size of the fight in the dog.
[Gen. Dwight D. Eisenhower, USA; speaking while serving as U.S. President, 31 January 1958]

There is nothing like seeing the other fellow run to bring back your courage.
    [Sir William Slim, British Army; *Unofficial History*, 1959]

I have always regarded the forward edge of the battlefield as the most exclusive club in the world.
    [LtGen. Sir Brian Horrocks, British Army; *A Full Life*, 1960]

In war there is no substitute for victory. *[and also]* Duty, Honor, Country. These three hallowed words reverently dictate what you *ought* to be, what you *can* be, what you *will* be.
    [Gen. Douglas MacArthur, USA; at West Point, 12 May 1962]

Victory is always possible for the person who refuses to stop fighting.
    [Napoleon Hill (1883-1970), American author]

The fundamental law of wartime negotiations: you negotiate with the enemy with your knee in his chest and your knife at his throat.
    [Gary J. Harris, military theorist]

Find, fix, fight, follow, finish.
    [universal military axiom for *destroying* the enemy]

The only men fit to live are those men who are not afraid to die.
    [sign at USN/USMC carrier-qualification training squadron VT-5, Pensacola, Florida, c 1964]

If your bayonet breaks, strike with the stock. If the stock gives way, hit with your fists. If your fists are hurt, bite with your teeth.
    [Gen. Makhail Dragomirov, Russian Army; *Notes for Soldiers*]

If you're in a fair fight, you didn't plan it properly.
    [CWO Nick Lappos, USA; speaking while serving as Chief R&D pilot, Sikorsky Aircraft Corp.]

A battle plan is good only until enemy contact is made.
    [Gen. H. Norman Schwarzkopf, USA; 1988]

Fight to fly, Fly to fight, Fight to win.
[motto of USN/USMC Fighter Weapons "Top Gun" School]

The finest steel has gone through the hottest fire. *[and also]* The lesson of all history warns us that we should negotiate only when our military superiority is so convincing that we can achieve our objectives at the conference table, and deny the aggressor theirs.
[Richard M. Nixon (1913-1994), U.S. President]

If you don't fight, you can't win. No guts, no glory.
[anonymous]

Nothing in life is more liberating than to fight for a cause larger than yourself.
[RAdm. John McCain, USN; *Faith of My Fathers*, 1999]

Glory is not an end in itself, but rather a reward for valor and faith.
[William J. Bennett, political observer; after reading the book by RAdm. John McCain, USN; *Faith of My Fathers*, 1999]

When America uses force in the world, the cause must be just, the goal must be clear, and the victory must be overwhelming.
[George W. Bush, presidential candidate (later U.S. President); addressing the Republican National Convention, 4 August 2000]

At the tip of the spear there is no room for second best
[Bell Helicopter Public Affairs, September 2000]

Do not fear the enemy, for, at the worst, he can only take your life. Instead, a wise warrior fears *the media*, for he knows the sniveling *media whores* may steal his honor.
[SSgt. Robert Johnson, USA; responding to a question from a high school student who had asked about a soldier's greatest fear in combat, in Fort Worth, Texas, August 2001]

I say to our enemies, God *may* show you mercy.
We will not.
[RAdm. John McCain, USN; also U.S. Senator, addressing the U.S. Senate, 12 September 2001]

Patriot Dreams

American Patriot! The words evoke thoughts of Paul Revere, Patrick Henry, and the American Revolution two-hundred-plus years ago. Yet, the meaning runs deeper than that.

Webster defines *patriot* as one "who loves, supports, and defends his country." By that definition a veritable host of patriots came to the aid of our fledgling republic during the long-ago struggle for American independence. Thomas Jefferson, George Washington, Nathan Hale, John Adams, Thomas Paine, and many others gave us our "government of the people."

All of those men are now dead and gone. Yet, a latter-day American Patriot reminds us that "Eternal vigilance is the price of freedom." The modern *Guidebook for Marines* explains the same premise in another way: "The price of freedom is not cheap."

History has shown that foreign despots will always plague the world: Lenin, Hitler, Mao, Tito, Stalin, Pol Pot, and their henchmen. Some barbarious tyrants like Tojo got the standard hangman's noose for their treacherous conduct. But Mussolini's countrymen went one better; they hung him *upside down*.

For others the ax has yet to fall. Idi Amin, who fed his opponents to crocodiles, survived to live in exile with the millions he plundered. Other tyrants still rule with an iron hand. Of course, the United States is not immune. Sometimes *our own* (Benedict Arnold, Bill Clinton, and their ilk) make a mockery of the trust vested in them.

A one-of-a-kind American icon was born in Winterset, Iowa, in 1907. His parents named him Marion Morrison, but the world would know him as **John Wayne** (1907-1979). He embodied all that is virtuous and good about his native land. He was a patriot, father, husband, humanitarian, actor, tycoon, role model, but most of all he became a genuine American hero. He has been called an "extra star on the American Flag." He *lived* the virtues that made him a legend. Seventeen years after his death, a Harris Poll revealed that he remains the most popular motion picture actor of all time. John Wayne once explained his love for his country:

> Sure I wave the American flag. Do you know of a better flag to wave? Sure I love my country with all her faults. I'm not ashamed of that. Never have been, never will be.

Fortunately each new generation has raised up American Patriots willing to sacrifice and serve. However, most of these modern-day patriots are not recognized as such. They are not like John Wayne. In our society, most of them are *invisible*.

The American Patriot of today is often the loyal legionnaire who dons his clothes with a prosthetic hand, without complaint. The patriot may be the stooped old Marine Warrior of yesteryear who bags groceries at the supermarket. Now palsied and slow, he never mentions the firestorm on Iwo Jima back in 1945, because he knows no one who could comprehend such indescribable horror. American Patriots are the thousands of Marine Warriors who went forth into battle for their country, and never returned.

Today's patriot is usually the common man, the average citizen, the next-door neighbor, the man who selflessly gave to his country and asked for nothing in return. The patriot of today may be a soft-spoken blue collar worker, a U.S. Marine veteran who charged into battle in Vietnam in 1968, or Kuwait in 1991, or Afghanistan in 2001, or Iraq in 2003, to restore freedom for people he would never know. Duty called. He answered.

Mao Tse-tung knew what he was talking about: "Power emanates from the barrel of a gun." Historically, after diplomacy and reason have failed, our country always turns to its modern-day American samurai, its elite Marine Warriors.

Remember: when enemies and terrorists threaten, it is always the *Marine Warrior*, not the politician, who ensures the survival of our society. It is always the *Marine Warrior*, not the news media, who guarantees our freedom of the press. When the flak flies it is the *Marine Warrior*, not the lawyer, who preserves our civil liberties.

In March 2001 a twelfth grade schoolgirl in Ohio stumbled across a few vague paragraphs in her history textbook. Her country had fought a war in faraway Vietnam, she learned. Why? Who had fought? What was at stake? Although she had always been a history buff, the schoolgirl could not recall the name of any

American involved in that conflict. Intrigued and challenged, she chose "Who Were The Heroes?" as the title of her senior thesis.

One Marine who fought in Vietnam answered the schoolgirl's public query. He explained that the heroes were just ordinary men. Actually, *boys* would be a more accurate description in most cases. But they were uniquely bound together. The U.S. Marines in Vietnam shared a common bond, the schoolgirl learned. They believed in each other. The old warrior explained two instances wherein Marines in Vietnam had selflessly risked their lives to aid their brothers-in-arms in peril. Then he added:

> There were thousands of such heroes. Simply stated, they believed in a cause greater than themselves . . . The heroes who survived are now in their fifties or sixties. You know them as fathers, uncles, neighbors, maybe teachers. They have jobs and families. They pay taxes and make our society function. They don't label themselves as heroes. Yet, they are American Patriots in every sense of the words. And deep down inside they still maintain that undying brotherly love for the men with whom they served in Vietnam thirty years or so ago. Without question, they are your heroes.

The same theme is interwoven into the storied battle history of the U.S. Marine Corps. All who have *earned the title* assume the American Patriot's mantle of responsibility. This Marine heritage runs deep. All Marines know that one of their own, Lt. Presley O'Bannon, was the first American Warrior to raise his country's flag in the Old World. The cherished warrior's anthem of the Corps, *The Marines' Hymn*, explains: "We fight our country's battles . . . ." The unique *Rifleman's Creed* includes the admonition: "My rifle and I are the defenders of my country."

The awe-inspiring Marine Corps War Memorial, the largest bronze monument on Earth, is based upon the world's most famous photograph. Further, it is topped by the flag of the United States of America. Patriotism! God, Country, and Corps! These virtues remain synonymous with the Warrior Culture of the U.S. Marines. For all Marine Warriors these virtues are inseparable, and patriotism never goes out of style.

Below are statements about patriotism and loyalty. Many come from the mouths of warriors. Others come from poets, historians, philosophers, heads of state, and others who understand and appreciate sacrificial devotion to one's native land:

Who here is so vile that will not love his country?
   [William Shakespeare (1564-1616), *Julius Caesar*]

Only a virtuous people are capable of freedom.
   [Benjamin Franklin, *Historical Review of Pennsylvania*, 1759]

Is life so dear, or peace so sweet, as to be purchased at the price of chains and slavery? Forbid it, Almighty God! I know not what course others may take, but as for me, give me liberty, or give me death!
   [Patrick Henry, American colonial statesman; to the Virginia Convention of Delegates, 23 March 1775]

Stand your ground, men. Don't fire unless fired upon. But if they mean to have a war, let it begin here.
   [Capt. James Parker, Continental Militia; to his "minute-men" before the British opened fire, 19 April 1775]

Those who expect to reap the blessings of liberty must, like men, undergo the fatigue of supporting it.
   [Thomas Paine, *The American Crisis*, 1776]

O ye that love mankind! Ye that dare oppose not only tyranny, but the tyrant, stand forth!
   [Thomas Paine, *Common Sense,* 1776]

. . . with a firm Reliance on the Protection of Divine Providence, we mutually pledge to each other our Lives, our Fortunes, and our sacred Honor.
   [Thomas Jefferson, excerpt from the United States' *Declaration of Independence*, 4 July 1776]

I only regret that I have but one life to lose for my country.
   [Capt. Nathan Hale, Continental Army; his last words before he was hanged as a spy by the British, 22 September 1776]

We, the people of the United States, in Order to form a more perfect Union, establish Justice, insure domestic Tranquility, provide for the common defence, promote the general Welfare, and secure the Blessings of Liberty to ourselves and our Posterity, do ordain and establish this Constitution for the United States of America.
  [James Madison, et al; the preamble to the *Constitution of the United States of America*, 17 September 1787]

The tree of liberty must be refreshed from time to time with the blood of patriots and tyrants.
  [Thomas Jefferson, American statesman; 13 November 1787]

You will never know how much it has cost my generation to preserve your freedom. I hope you will use it wisely.
  [John Adams (1735-1826), member of the Continental Congress, first U.S. Vice President, second U.S. President]

The only thing necessary for the triumph of evil is for good men to do nothing.
  [Edmund Burke (1729-1797), British parliamentarian]

In matters of principle, stand like a rock! *[and also]* I have sworn, upon the altar of God, eternal hostility against every form of tyranny over the mind of man.
  [Thomas Jefferson, American statesman; 23 September 1800]

Breathes there a man with soul so dead,
Who never to himself hath said,
This is my own, my native land!
  [Sir Walter Scott, *Lay of the Last Minstrel*, 1805]

And the star spangled banner in triumph shall wave,
O'er the land of the free and the home of the brave.
  [Francis Scott Key, American prisoner exchange negotiator; *The Defense of Fort McHenry* (later called *The Star Spangled Banner* and adopted as the U.S. National Anthem), during the British bombardment of Fort McHenry, 14 September 1814]

Our country! In her intercourse with foreign nations, may she always be in the right. But, our country, right or wrong!
   [Commodore Stephen Decatur, USN; at Norfolk, Virginia, 1816]

America is great because she is good. If America ever ceases to be good, America will cease to be great.
   [Alexis de Tocqueville, French historian; 1831]

My country, 'tis of thee, sweet land of liberty,
Of thee I sing; land where my fathers died,
Land of the pilgrims' pride, from every mountainside,
Let freedom ring!
   [Samuel F. Smith, *America*, 1832]

To the People of Texas and all Americans in the world . . . I call on you in the name of liberty, patriotism, & of everything dear in the American character, to come to our aid with all dispatch.
   [LtCol. William B. Travis, Texas Volunteer Militia; at the Alamo in southwest Texas, 24 February 1836]

Let us fly to arms, march to the battlefield, meet the foe, and give renewed evidence to the world that the arms of freemen, uplifted in defense of liberty and right, are irresistible. Now is the day, now is the hour, when Texas expects every man to do his duty. Let us show ourselves worthy to be free, and we shall be free.
   [Henry Smith, Governor of Texas; 2 March 1836]

One country, one constitution, one destiny. *[and also]* I was born an American; I live an American; I shall die an American. *[and also]* God grants liberty to those who love it and are always ready to guard and defend it.
   [Daniel Webster (1782-1852), U.S. Senator and orator]

If anyone attempts to haul down the American flag, shoot him on the spot.
   [John A. Dix, Secretary of the Treasury; 29 January 1861]

All I am, and all I have, is at the service of my Country.
   [LtGen. Thomas J. "Stonewall" Jackson, CSA; in a letter, 1861]

A thoughtful mind, when it sees a Nation's flag, sees not the flag only, but the Nation itself.
[Henry Ward Beecher, *The American Flag*, 1861]

One flag, one land, one heart, one hand, one nation, evermore.
[Oliver Wendell Holmes Jr., American jurist; 1862]

Fourscore and seven years ago our fathers brought forth on this continent a new nation, conceived in liberty, and dedicated to the proposition that all men are created equal.
[Abraham Lincoln, U.S. President; at the dedication of the National Cemetery at Gettysburg battlefield, 19 November 1863]

Dear Madam: I have been shown in the files of the War Department a statement of the Adjutant General of Massachusetts [which shows] that you are the mother of five sons who have died gloriously on the field of battle. I feel how weak and fruitless must be any words of mine which should attempt to beguile you from the grief of a loss so overwhelming. But I cannot refrain from tendering you the consolation that may be found in the thanks of the Republic they died to save. I pray that our heavenly Father may assuage the anguish of your bereavement, and leave you only the cherished memory of the loved and lost, and the solemn pride that must be yours to have laid so costly a sacrifice upon the altar of freedom.
[Abraham Lincoln, U.S. President; in a letter to Mrs. Lydia Bixbey, 21 November 1864 (read verbatim 134 years later in the motion picture, *Saving Private Ryan*, 1998)]

Abandon your animosities, and make your sons Americans.
[Gen. Robert E. Lee, CSA; after Appomattox, 1865]

The muster rolls on which the name and oath were written were pledges of honor -- redeemable at the gates of death. And those who went up to them, knowing this, are on the list of heroes.
[BGen. Joshua L. Chamberlain, USA; writing of the Union and Confederate volunteers during the American Civil War, 1866]

War is an ugly thing, but not the ugliest thing. The decayed and

degraded state of moral and patriotic feelings which thinks that nothing is worse than war is much worse. A man who has nothing for which he is willing to fight, nothing which is more important than his own personal safety, is a miserable creature and has no chance of being free -- unless made and kept so by the exertions of better men than himself.
   [John S. Mill, British philosopher; 1868]

There is something magnificent about having a country to love.
   [James Russell Lowell (1819-1891), American poet]

Eternal vigilance is the price of liberty.
   [Wendell Phillips (1811-1884), American orator]

A man's country is not a certain area of land . . . it is a principle; and patriotism is loyalty to that principle.
   [George William Curtis (1824-1892), American author]

I pledge allegiance to the Flag of the United States of America and to the Republic for which it stands, one nation, under God, indivisible, with liberty and justice for all.
   [Francis R. Bellamy, *Pledge to the Flag,* 1892 (the words "under God" were subsequently added)]

O beautiful for Patriot Dream, that sees beyond the years,
Thine alabaster cities gleam, undimmed by human tears!
America! America! God shed His grace on thee,
And crown thy good with brotherhood, from sea to shining sea.
   [Katherine L. Bates, *America the Beautiful,* 1893]

Liberty means responsibilities.
   [George Bernard Shaw, *Man and Superman,* 1903]

Our flag is our national ensign, pure and simple, behold it! Listen to it! Every star has a tongue, every stripe is articulate.
   [Robert C. Winthrop (1809-1894), U.S. Senator]

. . . I therefore believe it is my duty to my country to love it, to support its Constitution, to obey its laws, to respect its flag, and to

defend it against all enemies.
  [William Tyler Page, *The American Creed*, 1917]

Order without liberty, and liberty without order, are equally destructive.
  [Col. Theodore Roosevelt, USA, former President of the United States; *The Great Adventure*, 1918]

The meaning of America is not a life without toil. Freedom is not only bought with a great price, it is maintained by unremitting effort. *[and also]* Patriotism is easy to understand in America. It means looking out for yourself by looking out for your country.
  [Calvin Coolidge, U.S. President; in *The Price of Freedom*, 1924]

The only thing we have to fear is fear itself.
  [Franklin D. Roosevelt, U.S. President; 4 March 1933]

It is the love of country that has lighted, and that keeps glowing, the holy fire of patriotism.
  [J. Horace McFarland (1859-1948), political observer]

America is a passionate idea . . . America is a human brotherhood.
  [Max Lerner, *Actions and Passions*, 1949]

Only our individual faith in freedom can keep us free.
  [Gen. Dwight D. Eisenhower, USA; also U.S. President, 1952]

Patriotism is not short frenzied outbursts of emotion, but the tranquil and steady dedication of a lifetime.
  [Adlai E. Stevensen, American diplomat; 27 August 1952]

Live free or die.
  [motto of the State of New Hampshire]

I am an American, fighting in the armed forces which guard my country and our way of life. I am prepared to give my life in their defense.
  [Article I, Code of Conduct, U.S. Armed Forces; 1955]

Let every nation know, whether it wishes us well or ill, that we shall pay any price, bear any burden, meet any hardship, support any friend, oppose any foe, to assure the survival and success of liberty. *[and also]* Ask not what your country can do for you. Ask what you can do for your country.
    [John F. Kennedy, U.S. President; 20 January 1961]

The last time any of his fellow prisoners heard from him, Captain Versace was singing *God Bless America* at the top of his voice.
    [from posthumous Medal of Honor citation, Capt. Humbert Roque "Rocky" Versace, USA; a POW who was dragged from a bamboo cage and executed by the enemy on 26 September 1965]

. . . he was again wounded, this time in the right hand, which prevented him from operating his vitally needed machine gun. Suddenly and without warning, an enemy grenade landed in the midst of the few surviving Marines. Unhesitatingly and with complete disregard for his own personal safety, Corporal Barker threw himself upon the deadly grenade, absorbing with his own body the full and tremendous force of the explosion. In a final act of bravery he crawled to the side of a wounded comrade and administered first aid before succumbing to his wounds . . . He gallantly gave his life for his country.
    [Medal of Honor citation, LCpl. Jedh C. Barker, USMC; 1967]

. . . he sustained multiple fragmentation wounds from exploding grenades as he ran to an abandoned machine gun position . . . Corporal Maxam's position received a direct hit from a rocket propelled grenade, knocking him backwards and inflicting severe wounds to his face and right eye. Although momentarily stunned and in intense pain, Corporal Maxam courageously resumed his firing position and subsequently was struck again by small arms fire . . . the [enemy] threw hand grenades and directed recoilless rifle fire against him, inflicting two additional wounds. Too weak to reload his machine gun, Corporal Maxam fell to a prone position and valiantly continued to deliver effective fire with his rifle. After one and a half hours, during which he was hit repeatedly by fragments from exploding grenades and concentrated small arms fire, he succumbed to his wounds . . . He gallantly gave his life for

his country.
   [Medal of Honor citation, Cpl. Larry L. Maxam, USMC; 1968]

He insisted on giving his life so that forty of his fellow Marines might live and triumph. He had freely chosen loyalty above life.
   [1stLt. Michael Stick, USMC; speaking of Cpl. Larry L. Maxam, USMC; killed-in-action in Vietnam, 2 February 1968]

For those Marines who fought for it, freedom has a flavor that the protected will never know.
   [unidentified PFC, USMC; at Khe Sanh, Vietnam, April 1968]

We are *honored* to have had the *opportunity* to serve our country under difficult circumstances. We are profoundly *grateful* to our Commander-and-Chief and to our Nation for this day. *God bless America!*
   [Capt. Jeremiah A. Denton Jr., USN; former POW in North Vietnam for eight years, upon his release on 13 February 1973]

Let the Fourth of July always be a reminder that here in this land, for the first time, it was decided that man is born with certain God-given rights; that government is only a convenience created and managed by the people, with no power of its own except those voluntarily granted to it by the people. We sometimes forget that great truth, and we never should.
   [Ronald Reagan, U.S. President; 4 July 1981]

Sure, war is hell. But some things are worse than hell -- slavery being one.
   [RAdm. Jeremiah A. Denton Jr. (1924--) USN; also U.S. Senator, reflecting upon his eight years as a POW in North Vietnam]

The Marines knew they were fighting for freedom, and they had an enormous respect for basic American values.
   [SSgt. Arvin S. Gibson, USA; *In Search of Angels*, 1990]

You can just call me an American Patriot.
   [Maj. Harry R. "Bob" Mills, USMC; to a friend, 1991]

It is my heritage to stand erect, proud and unafraid. To think and act for myself, enjoy the benefit of my creations; to face the whole world and boldly say, "I am a free American."
[excerpt from *The Republican Creed*]

I swore to defend my nation against all enemies, foreign and domestic. It doesn't get any simpler. Stop trying to understand us.
[unidentified corporal, USMC; in *A Sense of Values*, 1994]

The red, white, and blue flag of the United States of America triumphantly fluttered in the stiff breeze atop Hill 881 North, deep in the heart of Indochina.
[Capt. Marion F. Sturkey, USMC; *Bonnie-Sue*, 1996]

The price of freedom is not cheap.
[Marine Corps Association, *Guidebook for Marines*, 1997]

We are, in fact, stewards of the past, present, and future.
[Gen. James L. Jones Jr., USMC (CMC); 10 November 2000]

I gave more to America than I ever took from America, and I am proud of it. Semper Fi! And, God bless you all.
[Col. Wayne Shaw, USMC; upon his retirement from the Corps]

America's freedom, and the values that protect us in the face of evil, are our great and glorious cause.
[RAdm. John McCain, USN; also U.S. Senator, September 2001]

Semper Fi, brothers! God bless the United States and the Corps!
[2ndLt. John E. Fales, USMC; 12 September 2001]

This will be a battle between good and evil . . . It will be an honor to fight for God, country, and the good of mankind.
[LCpl. Thomas C. Macedo, USMC; 20 September 2001]

There will never be another nation such as ours. Take good care of her. The fate of the world depends upon it.
[RAdm. John McCain, USN; also U.S. Senator, at the U.S. Naval Academy, 9 October 2001]

God has blessed America with much bounty and many fine men and women through the years, who have risked their lives -- then given them -- to preserve our liberty.
[Dr. David Russell, American Legion chaplain; 18 October 2001]

Vocal patriotism is a form of protest against terrorism.
[C. Welton Gaddy, in *Liberty*, 2002]

I do solemnly swear, or affirm, that I will support and defend the Constitution of the United States against all enemies, foreign and domestic; that I will bear true faith and allegiance to the same; that I will obey the orders of the President of the United States and the orders of the officers appointed over me, according to regulations and the Uniform Code of Military Justice. So help me God.
["Oath of Enlistment," U.S. Armed Forces (Public Law 87-751)]

I do solemnly swear, or affirm, that I will support and defend the Constitution of the United States against all enemies, foreign and domestic; that I will bear true faith and allegiance to the same; that I take this obligation freely, without any mental reservation or purpose of evasion; and that I will well and faithfully discharge the duties of the office on which I am about to enter. So help me God.
["Commissioning Oath," U.S. Armed Forces (40th Congress, 2d session, Chapter 139)]

Note: Any list of American patriotic statements should include the lyrics of *God Bless America*, and the lyrics of the refrain from *God Bless the USA*.

Irving Berlin wrote *God Bless America* in 1938, based upon similar lyrics he had composed in 1918. Kate Smith popularized the song by introducing it and singing it on her radio broadcast on Armistice Day (now, Veterans Day) later that year. Rights to the lyrics are held by a third party.

Lee Greenwood popularized the more recent song, *God Bless the USA*. Rights to the lyrics are held by a third party.

Somber Reflections on Combat

First, a few somber lines to set the stage:

> God of our fathers, known of old,
>   Lord of our far-flung battle line,
> Beneath whose awful hand we hold
>   Dominion over palm and pine --
> Lord God of Hosts, be with us yet,
> Lest we forget -- lest we forget!
> [Rudyard Kipling, *Recessional*, 1897]

Warfare and history can not be separated. In a sense, the history of mankind *is* the history of war. Those who have tasted combat know that war is obscene, terrible beyond mortal description.

Yet, throughout the centuries war has remained with us. Two thousand years ago St. Matthew cautioned the world that there will be "wars and rumours of wars" and that "nation shall rise against nation, and kingdom against kingdom . . . ." The history books have proved St. Matthew to be correct. Some nations resort to warfare out of need or greed or religious fervor. Other countries take up arms in self defense, to battle terrorism and tyranny, or to thwart assorted evils.

Historically the individual soldiers, the warriors, the centurions, the legionnaires, the individual combatants, have come from the ranks of the common man. Bound together by unity of cause and dedication to their Corps (by whatever name), they are revered by their countrymen. For the military elite, the famed Roman Legions of yesteryear or the Brotherhood of Marines of the past two centuries, warfare sometimes brought transient fame and glory. On the other hand, warfare also brought misery, privation, grief, agony, and indiscriminate death. War's toll is horror, hardship, cruelty, and madness.

The following words come from warriors and others who have seen the dark face of war. They know that fame and glory are fleeting. Combat is ugly, obscene, crippling, and insane. For the individual Marine Warrior, often the only victory that remains is eternal loyalty to his Corps and to his Marine brothers-in-arms, his friends for life:

Go tell the Spartans, thou that passeth by,
That here, obedient to the laws, we lie.
  [epitaph for the Spartan soldiers who fell in battle while holding the pass at Thermopylae, 480 BC]

War is sweet to those who have never experienced it.
  [Pindar (522-443 BC), Greek poet]

Only the dead have seen the end of war.
  [Plato (428-347 BC), Greek philosopher]

I did not mean to be killed today.
  [Vicomte de Turenne, a wounded French soldier; as he lay dying after the Battle of Salzbach, 1675]

These are the times that try men's souls. The summer soldier and the sunshine patriot will, in this crisis, shrink from the service of their country . . . Tyranny, like hell, is not easily conquered.
  [Thomas Paine, *The American Crisis*, 1776]

War is a rough, violent trade.
  [Johann C. Schiller, *The Piccolomini*, 1799]

Thank God I have done my duty.
  [the dying words of Viscount Horatio Nelson, RN; wounded aboard his *HMS Victory* off Cape Trafalgar, 21 October 1805]

I don't know what effect these soldiers will have on the enemy. But, by God, they terrify me!
  [Duke of Wellington, speaking of his own army, August 1810]

There is no uglier spectacle that two men with clenched teeth and hellfire eyes, hacking one another's flesh; converting precious

living bodies, and priceless human souls, into nameless putrescence.
[Thomas Carlyle, *Past and Present*, 1843]

On fame's eternal camping ground
Their silent tents are spread,
And glory guards with solemn round
The bivouac of the dead.
[Theodore O'Hara, *The Bivouac of the Dead*, 1847 (by an Act of Congress, to be displayed in every National Cemetery)]

Theirs not to make reply,
Theirs not to reason why,
Theirs but to do and die.
Into the valley of Death rode the six hundred.
[Alfred Tennyson, *The Charge of the Light Brigade*, 1854]

If a man had told me twelve months ago that men could stand such hardships, I would have called him a fool.
[Lt. James H. Langhorne, CSA; 8 January 1862]

No tongue can tell, no mind can conceive, no pen can portray, the horrible sights I witnessed this morning.
[Capt. John Taggart, USA; South Mountain, 17 September 1862]

Remember that the enemy you engage have no feelings of kindness or mercy towards you.
[MGen. Thomas C. Hindman, CSA; 7 December 1862]

It is well that war is so terrible -- we would grow too fond of it.
[Gen. Robert E. Lee, CSA; Fredericksburg, 13 December 1862]

Major, tell my father I died with my face to the enemy.
[Col. Issac E. Avery, CSA; his last words as he lay mortally wounded at Gettysburg, spoken to his adjutant, 2 July 1863]

Well, general, let's bury these poor men and say no more about it.
[Gen. Robert E. Lee, CSA; to MGen. A.P. Hill, CSA; in regard to the Confederate dead at Briscoe Station, 14 October 1863]

. . . We cannot dedicate, we cannot consecrate, we cannot hallow this ground. The brave men, living and dead, who struggled here have consecrated it far above our poor power to add or detract. The world will little note, nor long remember what we say here, but it can never forget what they did here.
[Abraham Lincoln, U.S. President; dedicating the National Cemetery at Gettysburg battlefield, 19 November 1863]

Don't worry. They couldn't hit an elephant at this dist . . . .
[the last words of Gen. John Sedgwick, USA; standing atop the parapet to direct artillery fire, and speaking to an aide who was pleading with him to take cover, just as he was shot through the neck and killed by a CSA sniper at Spotsylvania, 8 May 1864]

I had rather die than be whipped.
[MGen. J.E.B. "Jeb" Stuart, CSA; to his staff after he fell, mortally wounded, at Yellow Tavern, 11 May 1864]

War is cruelty and you cannot refine it.
[Gen. William T. Sherman, USA; in a letter to the Mayor of Atlanta, 12 September 1864]

None can realize the horrors of war, save those actually engaged. The dead lying all about, unburied to the last. My God! My God! What a scourge is war!
[Samuel Johnson, CSA; in a letter to his family, 1864]

When I was taken prisoner I weighed 165 pounds, and when I came out I weighed 96 pounds, and was considered stout compared to many I saw there.
[Pvt. A.S. Clyne, USA; a former POW at Andersonville, 1865]

There was never a time when, in my opinion, some way could not be found to prevent the drawing of the sword.
[Gen. Ulysses S. Grant (1822-1885), USA; also U.S. President]

There's only one truth about war: people die.
[Gen. Philip H. Sheridan (1831-1888), USA]

Not for fame or reward, not for place or rank,
Not lured by ambition or goaded by necessity;
But in simple obedience to duty as they understood it,
These men suffered all, sacrificed all,
Dared all - and died.
   [a eulogy by Rev. Randolph H. McKim, CSA chaplain; inscribed
   on the Confederate Memorial in Arlington National Cemetery]

There is many a boy here today who looks on war as all glory.
But, boys, war is Hell! . . . It is only those who have neither fired
a shot nor heard the shrieks and groans of the wounded who cry
aloud for blood, more vengeance, more destruction.
   [Gen. William T. Sherman, USA; addressing a patriotic gathering
   of military veterans and young men, 12 August 1880]

War loses a great deal of its romance after a soldier has seen his
first battle.
   [Col. John Mosby, CSA; *Mosby's War Reminiscences*, 1887]

Don't cheer, men. The poor devils are dying.
   [Capt. John W. Philip, USN; as his *USS Texas* passed the
   burning Spanish warship *Vizcaya* at Santiago, Cuba, 3 July 1898]

If I come out of this war alive, I will have more luck than brains.
   [Baron Capt. Manfred von Richthofen, German Flying Service
   ("The Red Baron" of Germany); in a letter to his mother, 1914]

The effects of the successful gas attack were horrible. I am not
pleased with the idea of poisoning men. Of course the entire world
will rage about it at first -- and then imitate us.
   [Rudolph Binding, *A Fatalist at War*, 1915; in regard to the
   German use of lethal gas at Vijfwege, Belgium, in April 1915]

I have seen war, and faced modern artillery, and I know what an
outrage it is against simple men.
   [Thomas M. Kettle, *The Ways of War*, 1915]

With a bullet through his head, he fell from an altitude of 9000

feet, a beautiful death.
[Baron Capt. Manfred von Richthofen, German Flying Service
("The Red Baron" of Germany); in a letter describing the death
of a friend, Count von Holck, near Verdun, France, 1 May 1916]

My God! Did we really send men to fight in that?
[LtGen. Sir Launcelot E. Kiggell, British Army; upon seeing the
mud and carnage after the Battle of Passchendaele, 1917]

What's the matter? Do you think that perhaps I will not return?
[Baron Capt. Manfred von Richthofen, German Flying Service
("The Red Baron" of Germany); to an airplane mechanic who
asked for his autograph before his final flight, 21 April 1918]

I have seen blood running from the wounded. I have seen men
coughing out their gassed lungs. I have seen the dead in the mud.
I have seen two hundred limping, exhausted men come out of the
line -- the survivors of a regiment of one thousand that went
forward forty-eight hours before.
[Franklin D. Roosevelt, Assistant Secretary of the Navy (later
U.S. President); with the U.S. Marines in France, June 1918]

War would end if the dead could return.
[Stanley Baldwin (1867-1947), British Prime Minister]

War, like any other racket, pays high dividends to the very few.
[MGen. Smedley D. Butler, USMC; 1933]

Enemy on island. Issue in doubt.
[last radio transmission from the besieged U.S. Marine garrison
on Wake Island, 23 December 1941]

Every day kill just one, rather than today five, tomorrow ten. Then
your nerves are calm and you can sleep good. You have your
drink in the evening and the next morning you are fit again.
[Col. Erich Hartmann, Luftwaffe; 352 air-to-air kills, WW II]

Older men declare war. But it is youth that must fight and die.
[Herbert Hoover, former U.S. President; 27 June 1944]

The beach was a sheet of flame backed by a wall of black smoke, as though the island was on fire . . . We piled out of our Amtrac amid blue-white Japanese machine gun tracers and raced inland.
[PFC Eugene B. Sledge, USMC; Peleliu, 15 September 1944]

Such a sight on that beach! Wrecked boats, bogged down jeeps, tanks burning, casualties scattered all over!
[Michael Kelecher, USN surgeon; Iwo Jima, February 1945]

How can I feel like a hero, when I hit the beach with two-hundred and fifty buddies, and only twenty-seven of us walked off alive?
[PFC Ira A. Hayes, USMC; after the battle, replying to a news media question about his role in raising the American flag atop Mt. Suribachi, Iwo Jima, on 23 February 1945]

All I wanted to get out of Iwo Jima was my fanny and dog tags.
[Cpl. Edward Hartman, USMC; after the battle, March 1945]

You never knew when you were drawing your last breath. You lived in total uncertainty, on the brink of the abyss, day after day.
[PFC Eugene B. Sledge, USMC; Okinawa, 1945]

Another improvement was that we built our gas chambers to accommodate two thousand people at one time.
[Rudolf Hess (1894-1987), Deputy Fuhrer of Nazi Germany; during his imprisonment after World War II]

A million deaths is a mere statistic.
[Josef W. Stalin (1879-1953), Russian dictator]

Consider yourselves already dead. Once you accept that idea, it won't be so tough.
[the fictitious World War II leader, Gen. Frank Savage, U.S. Army Air Corps; portrayed by Gregory Peck in the motion picture, *Twelve O'Clock High*, 1949]

The experience helped me realize how fragile life is. There could be two of you standing there . . . and in the next minute, only one.
[Pvt. Jack McCorkle, USMC; speaking years later of the fighting

at Chosin Reservoir, Korea, December 1950]

The staff intelligence officer handed me the pre-strike photos, the coordinates of the target, and told me to get on with it. He didn't mention that the bridges were defended by 56 radar-controlled antiaircraft guns.
[Capt. Paul N. Gray, USN; speaking years later of attacking the bridges at Toko-ri, Korea, on 12 December 1951]

The situation of the wounded is particularly tragic. They are piled on top of each other in holes that are completely filled with mud and devoid of any hygiene.
[Bernard B. Fall, *Hell in a Very Small Place*, 1966; quoting a French Army radio message from Dien Bien Phu, 5 May 1954]

The Legionnaire next to me disintegrated. Nothing was left of him except little pieces of raw meat. Death was spitting all around us. Men were falling like flies.
[a survivor of Dien Bien Phu in 1954, speaking years later]

The wounded were still lying there just like on the first day, intermingled with men who had died several days ago and were beginning to rot. They were lying there unattended, in the tropical sun, being eaten alive by the rats and the vultures. If only they had all been dead! *[and also]* As night fell over Dien Bien Phu the Legionnaires fixed bayonets in the ghostly light of the parachute flares and -- 600 against 40,000 -- walked into death.
[Bernard B. Fall, *Street Without Joy*, 1961]

The survivors would envy the dead.
[Nikita Khruschev, Premier of the Soviet Union; speaking of the possibility of global nuclear war, 1962]

By that time every Marine had been wounded. The living took the ammunition of the dead and lay under a moonless sky, wondering about the next assault.
[Capt. Francis J. West Jr., USMC; *Small Unit Action in Vietnam, Summer 1966*]

We were being attacked by a thousand men. We just couldn't kill them fast enough.

[Sgt. John J. McGinty, USMC; in *U.S. Marines in Vietnam, an Expanding War, 1966*]

One [survivor was] about eighteen, covered with gunpowder and dirt, black under the eyes. They were glassy. He was exhausted. Man, he looked bad, real bad. He said he had his bayonet fixed all night. I asked him if he had been scared, and he said, "Yeah." Right before daylight he had one bullet left. *One* bullet, just *one* bullet. So he started throwing rocks at the [enemy] in the dark. You know, tryin' to make 'em think the rocks were grenades. Only *one* bullet left. He was saving it for the final charge. He told me he realized he was gonna' die. Then, once he accepted that, he wasn't scared anymore.

[Capt. William T. Holmes, USMC; quoted in *Bonnie-Sue*, 1996, referring to a conversation in Vietnam on 9 August 1966]

He flew to Phu Bai, took off for Marble Mountain, and was never heard from again.

[Maj. Harry R. "Bob" Mills, USMC; speaking of his friend, Capt. William E. "Pappy" Johnson, USMC; MIA 6 October 1966]

He charged a machine gun bunker with hand grenades, trying to save some guys. He didn't have to do it. He got slaughtered. He had two kids.

[Capt. Otto H. Fritz, USMC; speaking years later of a sergeant in his company in Vietnam in October 1966]

Two machine guns keep up intense fire. NVA now have us almost surrounded. I have a terrible feeling I will never see my family again . . . Air strikes coming every 30 seconds. The ground trembles continuously. Once again I feel the end is near -- at least for me. I get an uncontrollable case of the shakes. I wonder if I ever had what it takes to be a Marine and conclude that I never did and don't now.

[Arnaud de Borchgrave, combat correspondent; "The Battle for Hill 400" in *Newsweek*, 10 October 1966]

Otto, you go ahead. I'm a dead man.
[1stLt. Steve Sayer, USMC; to his friend, 1stLt. Otto Fritz, USMC; the moment before Sayer was KIA, 10 December 1966]

I put my hand down, counted my fingers with my thumb, and went back to shooting. I was afraid to look at my arm.
[GySgt. Gareth L. "Red" Logan, USMC; writing years later of combat near Khe Sanh, Vietnam, on 25 April 1967]

Mike Company ceased to exist on that day; out of 190 men, only 26 were left standing.
[Austin Deuel, in *Vietnam Magazine*, describing 30 April 1967]

Where are those [expletive] choppers? All of my emergency medevacs are dead! All my priorities are now emergencies!
[HM3 Thomas Lindenmeyer, USN; Vietnam, 2 July 1967]

I don't think I'll be talking to you again. We are being overrun.
[last radio message from Capt. Warren O. Keneipp, USMC; his body, staked out and decapitated, was found 5 July 1967]

He was blown in half for a [expletive] place that had no strategic value, no military value, no sense to it, save to prove to Russia or China or North Vietnam or God or somebody that nineteen year old low and middle-class Americans would die for their country.
[a teenage U.S. Marine at Con Thien, Vietnam, 1967]

The lead aircraft disintegrated in the air. Two pilots, two crewmen, and one passenger were on board. There were no survivors.
[*HMM-262 Command Chronology*, 31 August 1967]

He was burning to death in the plane and couldn't get out. He was [screaming for] someone to tell his wife that he loved her, and for someone to shoot him.
[Ray Stubbe, USN chaplain; *The Final Formation*, 1995; quoting a witness to the death of a pilot at Khe Sanh on 23 August 1967]

We found part of Scribner's helmet with part of his head still inside . . . [it] looked like the rocket went off right in his lap.

There was nothing left.

[Ray Stubbe, USN chaplain; *The Final Formation*, 1995; quoting a Marine speaking of the death of a friend on 24 January 1968]

We huddled together in the bunker, shoulders high and necks pulled in to leave no space between helmet and flak jacket. There is no describing an artillery barrage. The earth shakes, clods of dirt fall from the ceiling, and shrapnel makes a repulsive singing through the air.

[John Donnelly, combat correspondent; "Drawing the Noose" at Khe Sanh, Vietnam, in *Newsweek*, 5 February 1968]

Everything I see is blown through with smoke, everything is on fire everywhere. It doesn't matter that memory distorts; every image, every sound comes back out of smoke and the smell of things burning. *[and also]* The Grunts themselves knew: the madness, bitterness, the horror and doom of it. *[and also]* The belief that one Marine was better than ten Slopes saw Marine squads fed in against known NVA platoons, platoons against companies, and on and on, until whole battalions found themselves pinned down and cut off. That belief was undying, but the Grunt was not.

[Michael Herr, *Dispatches*, 1968]

Sometimes in the morning we'd see three or four hundred bodies out along the wire. *[and also]* Every inch of the runway was zeroed in, and if an airplane tried to land they just walked artillery rounds right up the center line. *[and also]* They had the glide slope zeroed in with .50 caliber machine guns and they knew exactly where to shoot to hit you on it. They'd just listen for you and start laying fire down the glide slope. If you were on it, you were drilled.

[LtCol. David L. Althoff, USMC; "Helicopter Operations at Khe Sanh" in *Marine Corps Gazette*, May 1969]

It was raining. I was a replacement for a company commander who had been killed the night before. The tank lurched to a halt. I jumped off, walked over to a hole and asked, "Where is the CP?" A filthy, soaking wet Marine continued bailing out his hole with a C-ration can and answered, "You're in it." I asked for the battalion

commander. He answered, "You're looking at him."
[Maj. Matthew P. Caulfield, USMC; writing "India Six" about combat in Vietnam, in *Marine Corps Gazette*, July 1969]

(1) There was no conversation, just heavy grunting as they beat him with their fists . . . there was a steady "thump, thump." The guards had become more agitated and were beating his head against his wooden pallet. *[and also]* (2) Jerry, I'm in bad shape. They are giving me almost nothing to eat. I'm down to a hundred pounds and I haven't crapped in twenty-six days. I don't remember how long I've been in irons, but it's been weeks. I don't know whether I can make it.
[RAdm. Jeremiah A. Denton Jr., USN (later a U.S. Senator); (1) describing the beating of a fellow POW, and (2) paraphrasing a fellow POW's words, *When Hell Was in Session*, 1976]

Samuels looked down and saw that his left leg was flipped crazily to one side midway down below the knee. There was no way his leg could be lying there like that and still be -- still be attached.
[C.D.B. Bryan, *Friendly Fire*, 1976]

War runs best on evil . . . How else can you convince boys to kill one another day after day? *[and also]* War is not killing. Killing is the easiest part of the whole thing. Sweating twenty-four hours a day, seeing guys drop all around you of heatstroke, not having food, not having water, sleeping only three hours a night for weeks at a time, that's what war is. *[and also]* I'd pray for a firefight, just so we could stop walking. *[and also]* Vietnam was a Neverland, outside of time and space, where little boys didn't have to grow up. They just grew old before their time.
[Mark Baker, *NAM*, 1981]

It was a slaughter. No better than lining people up on the edge of a ditch and shooting them in the back of the head. I was doing it enthusiastically.
[unidentified helicopter gunner, quoted in *NAM*, 1981]

There was a Christmas truce, but we flew anyway. I couldn't get over how bizarre it was. We would decide to stop killing each

other for a few days, and then start again. *[and also]* I felt like a worm on a string. The tracers rushed past us like a line of UFOs in a hurry. I promised God that I would quit smoking and I would never touch a whore, not even get a hand job, and I would believe in Him if He would only let me live.
   [WO Robert Mason, USA; *Chickenhawk*, 1984]

The enduring emotion of war, when everything else has faded, is comradeship. A comrade in war is a man you can trust with anything, because you have trusted him with your life. *[and also]* In war the line between life and death is gossamer thin; there is joy, true joy, in being alive when so many around you are not.
   [William Broyles Jr., "Why Men Love War" in *Esquire*, 1984]

The POWs I saw were very thin; they were covered with scabies -- there was just skin and bones left on them. They could hardly walk, yet they were forced to carry wood from the forests. They often fell down. They were beaten by the guards.
   [unidentified South Vietnamese soldier, in *Life on the Line*, 1988]

The only thing clean borne of this life is cruelty and filth.
   [unidentified British private, quoted in *Eye Deep in Hell: Trench Warfare in World War I*, 1989]

I now know why men who have been to war yearn to reunite. Not to tell war stories or look at old pictures. Not to laugh or weep. Comrades gather because they long to be with men who once acted their best, men who suffered and sacrificed, who were stripped raw, right down to their humanity. I did not pick these men. They were delivered by fate and the U.S. Marine Corps. But I know them in a way that I know no other men. I have never given anyone such trust. They were willing to guard something more precious than my life. They would have carried my reputation, the memory of me. It was part of the bargain we all made, the reason we were so willing to die for one another.
   [Michael Norman, Marine veteran; *These Good Men*, 1990]

Every time we lost a pilot or crewmember, we lost so much more

than just a life. We lost a friend.
   [Capt. Bruce R. Lake, USMC; *1500 Feet Over Vietnam*, 1990]

Thirty, forty, maybe fifty Marines lay twisted along both sides of the road, clumped atop each other in spots, their weapons and gear strewn down the middle of the road . . . a slaughterhouse.
   [William K. Nolan, *Operation Buffalo*, 1991]

Death is so commonplace it doesn't shock you anymore. *[and also]* Flying in the night rain with fog was a death warrant. *[and also]* The [dead] pilot had committed the unforgivable error of flying his aircraft into a cloud with a mountain hidden inside.
   [LtCol. H. Lee Bell, USMC; *1369*, 1992]

He was just a kid, as was I. He confided to me that he had never even kissed a girl before . . . Unfortunately, he never got the chance. I think his mother would be happy to know that only God and her [sic] ever knew the tenderness of his kiss.
   [Ray Stubbe, USN chaplain; *The Final Formation*, 1995; quoting a friend of PFC Bruce Cunningham, USMC; KIA in Vietnam]

Our government does not want America to know that our darkest secret is that we killed many Americans in cold blood. They were tortured to death in prison, or simply killed outright from fear they would try to escape. And our leaders are afraid to admit this. They were tortured to death here in Hanoi.
   [LtCol. Nguyen Van Thi, Vietnamese Army; quoted in *Inside Hanoi's Secret Archives: Solving the MIA Mystery*, 1995]

We did unspeakable things we won't now admit -- not even to ourselves. We held the God-like power of life and death in our hands. After the war we suppressed the killer instinct, usually hiding it behind a low-key facade of casual humor. But the evil still lives in us, lurking somewhere just beneath the surface.
   [Capt. Marion F. Sturkey, USMC; in a handwritten memoir for the "Epilog" of *Bonnie-Sue,* 1996]

War is a cruel game, a brutal game, a deadly game. *[and also]* The overwhelming sensation was that of deafening noise and bedlam.

No one could hear the individual weapons firing, the bombs exploding, the shouts and screams. There was only a continuous cacophony, a horrible roar. *[and also]* It was surreal, unbelievable, macabre, horrible. Angry orange flames and jet black smoke now billowed out behind the doomed helicopter as it headed for the valley floor. *[and also]* Plummeting earthward, Joe saw blue sky through the plexiglass in front of him in one instant, then land, then water, then sky again. He remembers screaming incoherently, because he knew he was going to die.

    [Capt. Marion F. Sturkey, USMC; *Bonnie-Sue*, 1996]

Men caught in the killing zone became instant dogmeat. *[and also]* Marine helicopter crews who survived an entire tour unscathed led charmed lives. Enemy gunfire downed 1,777 helicopters during the first five years of the war; others returned to base shot to splinters.

    [Col. Joseph H. Alexander, USMC; *A Fellowship of Valor*, 1997]

Every modern amphibious operation is, by definition, a catastrophe waiting to happen.

    [Col. Joseph H. Alexander, USMC; in *The Marines*, 1998]

Marines learned the realities of the Western Front: mud, shelling, barbed wire, rats, corpses in various states of disintegration, an almost invisible enemy, trench raids, gas attacks . . . .

    [BGen. Edwin H. Simmons, USMC; in *The Marines*, 1998]

Now we're older, fatter, grayer. We're fathers and grandfathers, and most of us fly helicopters only in our dreams. But we lived through it all [the Vietnam War], lived to tell about it, if only to tell each other, and that's not bad.

    [Cpl. Lou Sessinger, USMC; writing of USMC helicopter crews in "One Organization Worth Joining," 14 October 1999]

Sweat gathered inside our rubber boots, and when we pulled off a sock, frozen skin came with it. Sleep was out of the question. Training enabled us to keep fighting. Surrounded as we were, there was no rear, no front, no flank.

    [Sgt. Werner "Ronnie" Reininger, USMC; writing years later of the fighting near Hagaru-ri, Korea, in *Leatherneck*, January 2001]

Second place was a body bag.
  [Capt. Roger A. Herman, USMC; in *The Log Book*, 2001]

I watched Marines die face down in the mud protecting freedom.
  [Col. Oliver North, USMC; 21 September 2001]

Beware of war hawks who never served in the military.
  [James Bradford, in *USA Today*, 17 September 2002]

I came across the body of the old man with the cane. He had a massive wound in the back of his head. He died on his back, looking at the sky, and his body was covered with flies.
  [Peter Maass, writing "Good Kills" about U.S. Marines in Iraq, in the *New York Times Magazine*, 20 April 2003

No sane person who has ever been to war wants to go to another.
  [Col. Oliver North, USMC; 29 May 2003]

. . . and for the history books . . . .

One U.S. Marine, Cpl. Daniel D. "Dan" Dulude, has been awarded the Silver Star on *two consecutive* days:
  1. Hill 861 near Khe Sanh, Vietnam, on 24 April 1967
  2. Hill 700 near Khe Sanh, Vietnam, on 25 April 1967

One U.S. Marine, LtGen. Lewis B. "Chesty" Puller, has been awarded the Navy Cross *five* times:
  1. Nicaragua, for action during June and July 1930
  2. Nicaragua, for action during 20-30 September 1932
  3. Guadalcanal, for the night of 24-25 October 1942
  4. Cape Gloucester, for 2-3 January 1944
  5. near Chosin, Korea, during November-December 1950

Marine Corps History

Origin of the United States Marine Corps: Fighting men on ships date back to the Phoenicians and Greeks around 500 BC. They served as boarding parties, and as infantry when securing land bases and harbors. The Romans later adopted this military strategy. Eventually, so did the British, and in 1664 the British Admiralty named its *soldiers of the sea* the "Regiment of Marines."

In the fledgling American colonies on 10 November 1775, the Continental Congress met in Tun Tavern in Philadelphia. This new renegade congress resolved:

> That two Battalions of Marines be raised consisting of one Colonel, two Lieutenant Colonels, two Majors & Officers as usual in other regiments, that they consist of an equal number of privates with other battalions; that particular care be taken that no person be appointed to office or enlisted into said Battalions, but such as are good seamen, or so acquainted with maritime affairs as to be able to serve to advantage by sea.

The new *Continental Marines* set up their recruiting station in Tun Tavern (see the next two sub-chapters). Led by their Commandant, in March 1776 they conducted their first amphibious assault against the British in the Bahamas. The Marines served as naval infantry aboard Continental Navy ships and as expeditionary forces throughout the Revolutionary War. But when the Treaty of Paris ended the war in 1783, the Continental Navy and the Continental Marines faded out of existence.

Fifteen years later the new United States and France prepared to lock military horns. Consequently, the U.S. Congress formally established the *United States Marine Corps* on 11 July 1798. Since that time the U.S. Marines have conducted over 300 assaults on foreign shores. Marines have formed the point-of-the-spear in thousands of battles throughout the world. Through their prowess in combat, their 'elan, and their gungy *esprit de corps*, U.S.

Marines have fought their way into the legendary Valhalla for Warriors -- universal recognition as the premier warriors on Earth, the world's Warrior Elite.

Tun Tavern: Ask any Marine. Just ask. He will tell you that the Marine Corps was *born* in Tun Tavern on 10 November 1775. Beyond that, the Marine's recollection for detail will probably get fuzzy. Consequently, here is the straight scoop:

In 1685, roughly 90 years before the American Revolution, Samuel Carpenter built a huge "brew house" in Philadelphia. He located his tavern on the waterfront at the corner of Water Street and Tun Alley. The old English word *tun* means a cask, barrel, or keg of beer. Therefore, with his new beer tavern on Tun Alley, Carpenter elected to christen the proud new waterfront brewery with a logical name, Tun Tavern.

The new brewery quickly gained a reputation for serving fine beer. Beginning 47 years later in 1732, the first meetings of the St. John's No. 1 Lodge of the Grand Lodge of the Masonic Temple were held in the tavern (even today, the Masonic Temple of Philadelphia recognizes Tun Tavern as the birthplace of Masonic teachings in America). A famous American statesman, Benjamin Franklin, became the third Grand Master of the Lodge. While enjoying libations in the tavern, Franklin once wrote: "Beer is living proof that God loves us and wants us to be happy."

Roughly ten years later in the early 1740s, the new proprietor expanded Tun Tavern and gave the addition a new name, "Peggy Mullan's Red Hot Beef Steak Club at Tun Tavern." The new restaurant became a smashing commercial success. In 1747 the St. Andrews Society, a charitable group dedicated to assisting poor immigrants from Scotland, was founded in the tavern. By then the brewery had become a popular meeting place in Philadelphia.

Nine years later, then Col. Benjamin Franklin organized the Pennsylvania Militia. He used Tun Tavern as a gathering place to recruit a regiment of soldiers to march into battle against the Indian uprisings that were plaguing the American colonies. George Washington, Thomas Jefferson, and the Continental Congress later met in Tun Tavern as the American colonies prepared to fight for independence from the English Crown.

On 10 November 1775 (the revered Marine Corps birthday) the Continental Congress commissioned Samuel Nicholas to raise two Battalions of Marines. Later that very day, Nicholas *set up shop* in Tun Tavern. He appointed Robert Mullan, then the proprietor of the tavern, to the job of chief Marine Recruiter. Mullen recruited from his place of business at Tun Tavern. Prospective recruits flocked to the tavern, lured by (1) cold beer, (2) gung-ho rhetoric, and (3) the opportunity for adventure in the new *Continental Marines*, forerunner of the U.S. Marine Corps.

So, yes, the Marine Corps was indeed *born* in Tun Tavern. Needless to say, both the Marine Corps and the tavern thrived during this new relationship.

Tun Tavern still "lives" today at a new location, renamed as Tun Tavern Brewery and Restaurant. And -- you guessed it -- Tun Tavern Beer remains the patrons' libation of choice.

First Marine Corps Recruiting Poster: The Continental Marines were born in Tun Tavern on 10 November 1775. Under the direction of Capt. Nicholas, Robert Mullen set up his recruiting station in the tavern. Publicity? Recruiting posters?

Mullen used cold beer as his main recruiting tool. History tells us that this proved to be a truly *outstanding* idea. As a recruiting tool, cold beer worked wonders!

Two months later in January 1776, six months before the *Declaration of Independence*, the first **known** recruiting poster rolled off the press. In the language of the day, it enticed "every Lord of Spirit" to enlist in the Continental Marines.

Seventeen dollars was the standard enlistment incentive. Those who induced a friend to enlist got three dollars, but the main inducement to enlist was the prospect of "Prize Money." The fledgling Continental Navy ships would act as *privateers* -- a polite word for *pirates*. Any captured ship would be looted. The bounty would be shared by the crew, including the Continental Marines.

There was not much thought given to "truth in advertising." Glory and prize money reigned supreme. Plus, prospective recruits were promised nine drinks ("Three Times Three, you shall drink") at Tun Tavern. Nine mugs of cold beer worked every time! The original Continental Marines Recruiting Poster wording is quoted below. Note the unique language of the late 1700s:

****

Great Encouragement
AMERICAN REVOLUTION
What a Brilliant Prospect does this Event hold out to every Lord of Spirit, who is enclined [sic] to try his Fortune in that highly renound [sic] Corps,
THE CONTINENTAL MARINES
When every Thing that swims the Seas must be a
PRIZE!
Thousands are at this moment endeavoring to get on Board Privateers, where they serve without Pay or Reward of any kind whatsoever: so certain does their Chance appear of enriching themselves by **PRIZE MONEY!** What an enviable Station then must the **CONTINENTAL MARINE** hold, -- who with far superior Advantages to these, has the additional benefit of liberal Pay, and plenty of the best Provisions, with a good and well appointed Ship under him, the Pride and Glory of the Continental Navy; surely every Man of Spirit must blush to remain at Home in Inactivity and Indolence, when his Country needs his Assistance.

When then can he have such fair opportunity of reaping Glory and Riches, as in the Continental Marines, a Corps daily acquiring new Honors and here, when once embarked in American Fleet, he finds himself in the midst of Honor and Glory, surrounded by a few of fine Fellow[s], Strangers to Fear, and who strike Terror through the Hearts of their Enemies wherever they go! He has likewise the inspiring idea to know that while he scours the Oceans to protect the Liberty of these states, that the Hearts and good Wishes of the whole American peoples attend him: pray for his success, and participate in his Glory!! Lose no time then, my fine Fellows, in embracing the glorious Opportunity that awaits you; YOU WILL RECEIVE
SEVENTEEN DOLLARS BOUNTY,
And on your arrival at Head Quarters, be comfortably and genteely [sic] CLOTHED, -- And spirited young BOYS of a promising Appearance, who are Five Feet Six Inches high, **WILL RECEIVE TEN DOLLARS**, and equal Advantages of

PROVISIONS and CLOTHING with the Men. And, those who wish only to enlist for a limited Service, shall receive a Bounty of **SEVEN DOLLARS**, and Boys FIVE. In Fact; the Advantages which the MARINE [enjoys], are too numerous to mention here, but among many, it may not be amiss to state -- That if he has a WIFE or aged PARENT, he can make them an Allotment of half his PAY; which will be regularly paid without any Trouble to them, or to whomsoever he may directs [sic] that being well Clothed and Fed on Board Ship, the Remainder of his PAY and **PRIZE MONEY** will be clear in Reserve for the Relief of his Family or his own private Purposes. The Simple Young Man on his Return to Port, finds himself enabled to cut a Dash on Shore with his GIRL and his GLASS, that might be envied by a Nobleman. -- Take Courage then, seize the Fortune that awaits you, repair to the MARINE RENDEZVOUS, where in a FLOWING BOWL of PUNCH, and Three Times Three, you shall drink.

Long Live The United States, and Success to the Marines.

The Daily Allowance of a Marine when embarked is -- One Pound of BEEF or PORK, -- One Pound of Bread, -- Flour, Raisins, Butter, Cheese, Oatmeal, Molasses, Tea, Sugar, & etc. And a Pint of the best Wine, or half a Pint of the best RUM or BRANDY; together with a Pint of LEMONADE. They have liberty in warm Countries, a plentiful Allowance of the choicest FRUIT. And what can be more handsome than the Marines' Proportion of PRIZE MONEY, when a Sergeant shares equal with the First Class of Petty Officers, such as Midshipmen, Assistant Surgeons, & which is Five Shares each; a Corporal with the Second Class, which is Three Shares each; and the Private with the Able Seaman, one Share and a Half each.

[Those] Desiring greater Particulars, and a more full Account of the many Advantages of this invaluable Corps, apply to CAPTAIN MULLAN, at TUN TAVERN, where the Bringer of a Recruit will receive **THREE DOLLARS**.

Common Nicknames for U.S. Marines: Over the years, U.S. Marines have accumulated a variety of nicknames or monikers. Many are foolish, some are obscene, and most such terms have not survived the test of time. Yet, other terms for Marine Warriors are rooted in the history and battle lore of the Brotherhood of Marines:

Leatherneck: The gungy nickname, *Leatherneck*, has become a universal moniker for a U.S. Marine. The term originated from the wide and stiff leather neck-piece that was part of the Marine Corps uniform from 1798 until 1872. This leather collar, called *The Stock*, was roughly four inches high and had two purposes. In combat, it protected the neck and jugular vein from cutlass slashes. On parade, it kept a Marine's head erect. The term is so widespread that it has become the name of the Marine Corps Association monthly magazine, *Leatherneck*.

Gyrene: Around 1900, members of the U.S. Navy began using *Gyrene* as a jocular derogatory reference to U.S. Marines. Instead of being insulted, the Marines loved it. The term became common by World War I and has been extensively used worldwide since that time.

Jarhead: For roughly 50 years, sailors had little luck in their efforts to insult Marines by calling them *Gyrenes*. During World War II, sailors tried a new tactic. They began referring to Marines as *Jarheads*. Presumably the high collar on the Marine uniform made a Marine's head look like it was sticking out of the top of a jar. Marines were not insulted. Instead, they embraced the new moniker as a term of utmost respect.

Devil Dogs: The German Army coined this term of respect for U.S. Marines during World War I. In the summer of 1918 the German Army was driving toward Paris. The French Army was in full retreat. In a desperate effort to save Paris, the newly arrived U.S. Marines were thrown into the breach. In the summer of 1918, in bitter fighting lasting for weeks, Marine Warriors repeatedly repulsed the German onslaught in Belleau Wood. The German drive toward Paris slowed down, sputtered, fizzled, and then died.

Then the Marines counterattacked. They swept the Germans back out of Belleau Wood, and Paris had been saved. The tide of war turned. Five months later Germany would be forced to accept an armistice.

The battle tenacity and fury of the U.S. Marines had stunned the Germans. In their official reports they called the Marines "teufel hunden." In the German language, teufel hunden are *Devil Dogs*, the ferocious mountain dogs of Bavarian folklore.

Soldiers of the Sea: A traditional and functional term for "naval infantry," or Marines, dating back to the British in the 1600s.

Marine Corps Emblem and Marine Corps Seal: The Marine Corps Emblem has evolved over time. Initially the Continental Marines adopted an emblem similar to that used by the Royal Marines. In 1776 it appeared as a *foul anchor* (an anchor with one or more turns of chain around it) made of pewter or silver.

Changes came with the passing years. Most notably, in 1834 a brass eagle was added atop the anchor. The next few years brought black cockades, scarlet plumes, and yellow bands and tassels. By 1859 the emblem included a United States shield, a half wreath, a bugle, and the letter *M*.

Enough of that! In 1868 the Commandant, BGen. Jacob Zeilin, approved the Marine Corps emblem that has survived until today with only minor changes. The emblem is based upon a globe depicting the western hemisphere, intersected by a foul anchor and topped by a spread eagle -- the *eagle, globe, and anchor*. The eagle holds in its beak a ribbon inscribed with the motto of the Corps, *Semper Fidelis*. Uniform ornaments omit the ribbon.

The general design of the Marine Corps emblem has been heavily influenced by the "Globe and Laurel" of the British Royal Marines. Historically, the globe signifies worldwide service. The eagle, like the Corps itself, indicates supremacy. The anchor reflects the amphibious nature of the Corps.

The Marine Corps Seal incorporates the Marine Corps Emblem. The seal was designed by the Marine Corps Uniform Board and adopted by Presidential Executive Order No. 10538 on 22 June 1954. On the seal, the emblem is surrounded by the Marine Corps colors, scarlet and gold. These colors are, in turn, enclosed by Navy blue and gold, signifying the elite Marine Corps role within the Department of the Navy. Within the outer band of the seal are the words: "DEPARTMENT OF THE NAVY - UNITED STATES MARINE CORPS."

Marine Warriors have a habit of plastering their Marine Corps Seal, in decal form, on almost everything: wall lockers, vehicles, desks, buildings, combat equipment -- whatever! When you are the best of the best, you want the whole world to know it. And when you are the world's Warrior Elite, it is hard to be humble.

Mameluke Sword and NCO Sword: At the beginning of the 1800s the United States was a defenseless country. Nonetheless, it maintained an active maritime trade with Europe. Unfortunately, *piracy* was the main international growth industry at the time. The battle between the new United States and the Mediterranean-based pirates would become known as the "Barbary Wars."

An international coalition (sound familiar?) assembled to attack the pirate stronghold of Derna, Tripoli, in what is now Libya. A force of eight U.S. Marines and about 500 mercenaries landed at Alexandria, Egypt. Led by a Marine officer, 1stLt. Presley N. O'Bannon, they trekked for 50 days across the desert. In spite of mutinies, which were squelched by the Marines, and desertions along the way, this rag-tag band reached the pirates' city-fortress of Derna on 27 April 1805.

The Marines and mercenaries formed a line of battle. Then they attacked. The assault degenerated into a wild and bloody melee. Sabres flashed. Muskets belched smoke and lead. Slowly the attackers fought their way toward Derna's main defenses, the high city walls ringed with cannon.

After three hours of combat the defenders had been rocked by heavy casualties. They lost their taste for battle, turned tail, and fled into the open desert. Lt. O'Bannon, who had lost three Marines and a hundred or so mercenaries, accepted the surrender of the fortress commander. O'Bannon then hoisted the American flag over the fortress -- the first time the American flag had been raised in the Old World.

The audacity and ferocity of the attack amazed a Mameluke desert warlord. He was so impressed that he gave his jeweled scimitar to O'Bannon, the "ultimate warrior."

Back in the United States, newspapers from Savannah to Boston soon touted O'Bannon's Marines and their conquest in Tripoli. They extolled (and exaggerated) the exploits of O'Bannon and his now-famous Mameluke Sword.

Swept up in the patriotic fever, Marine officers began purchasing imitation Mameluke Swords for themselves. Bowing to public pressure in 1825, the Marine Corps mandated new Mameluke Swords -- without the jewels -- for all Marine Corps officers. To this day a Marine officer's Mameluke Sword is recognized by its ivory grips, brass guard, curved blade, and silver scabbard.

Later, Marine noncommissioned officers also got into the sword game. The warrior-oriented Marine Corps issued distinctive sabers of a different design to its NCOs. Today the elite Marine Corps remains the only American military service that issues ceremonial sabres to its NCOs.

Most U.S. Marine NCOs subtly point out that their sabres are not necessarily restricted to the parade ground. Hard-charging Marine NCOs maintain a razor-sharp edge on their sabre blades. Anyone not suitably impressed can be *dispatched* in short order.

History of *The Marines' Hymn*: The U.S. Army, the U.S. Navy, and the U.S. Air Force all have their own songs.

U.S. Navy: *Anchors Aweigh* was written in 1906 by Lt. Charles Zimmerman and midshipman Alfred Miles. Initially the song was a tribute to the Naval Academy Class of 1907. Various people revised it later, trying to weed out some of the nonsense. Another midshipman, Royal Lovell, penned the final stanza in 1926. *Anchors Aweigh* has a snappy little tune, but no one is sure what the words imply. The original first stanza in 1906 had dealt solely with the game of football. Even today, the song offers a bittersweet "farewell to college joys." The lyrics end by "wishing you a happy voyage home." Some musical experts claim that *Anchors Aweigh* is a ballad for football players who like sailboats. But no one really knows for certain.

U.S. Army: Soldiers loved the peppy tune of *The Caisson Song*. Edmund Gruber had written the original lyrics in the Philippines during World War I. Naturally, since most of the fighting was 8000 miles away in Europe, Gruber made only a passing reference to warfare. Yet, he was careful to be "politically correct." He may have sought the help of first grade students in composing the lyrics. The juvenile "hi, hi, hee" is a dead giveaway.

By 1948 caissons had become outdated. The Army kept the tune of *The Caisson Song*, changed "hi, hi, hee" to "Hi, Hi, Hey," added a few stanzas, and renamed the anthem, *The Army Goes Rolling Along* -- but most soldiers still prefer *The Caisson Song*.

U.S. Air Force: There was no U.S. "Air Force" in 1938. But in that year *Liberty Magazine* sponsored a contest for an official song for the Army Air Corps. The magazine received 757 entries. A group of Army Air Corps wives (yes, believe it or not, *wives*) selected the entry from Robert Crawford, *Off We Go into the Wild Blue Yonder*.

After World War II the Army Air Corps evolved into the new U.S. Air Force. This fledgling flying club adopted *Off We Go'* as their official song. It suited the illusionary nature of the new Wild-Blue-Yonder-Wonders with references to "those who love the vastness of the sky" and the fictitious "rainbow's pot of gold." The final stanza speaks of the "gray haired wonder," an admirable gesture of non-discrimination for the new civilianized Air Force.

These three songs, (1) *Anchors Aweigh*, (2) *The Army Goes Rolling Along*, and (3) *Off We Go into the Wild Blue Yonder*, are often played at public events. They obviously delight members and advocates of the affected service: Navy, Army, or Air Force. When their song is played, sailors, soldiers, and zoomies leap to their feet, shout, cheer, clap their hands, and jive with the music. They have a jolly time, almost like a high school pep rally.

U.S. Marine Corps: The elite Corps of Marines is the military band of brothers dedicated to warfighting. The proud Brotherhood of Marines is guided by principles, values, virtues, love of country, and its Warrior Culture. This brotherhood of American Patriots has no song. Instead, Marine Warriors have a *hymn*. When *The Marines' Hymn* is played, United States Marines stand at attention. They reverently demonstrate their pride in their brothers-in-arms, their Corps, their fighting heritage, and their hymn.

The Marines' Hymn is a tribute to Warriors. Marines fought their way into the castle at Chapultepec and gave us the "halls of Montezuma." Marine Warriors stormed fortress Derna, raised the American flag, and gave us "the shores of Tripoli." Marines exist for the purpose of warfighting. Fighting is their role in life. They "fight for right and freedom" and "to keep our honor clean." They fight "in the air, on land, and sea." The Marine Corps is Valhalla for Warriors. U.S. Marines need no *song*. They have a *hymn*.

Ironically, no one knows who wrote the hymn, which was in widespread use by the mid-1800s. Col. A.S. McLemore, USMC, spent several years trying to identify the origin of the tune. In 1878 he told the leader of the Marine Band that the tune had been adopted from the comic opera *Genevieve de Barbant*, by Jaques Offenback. Yet, others believe the tune originated from a Spanish folk song. Whatever! Regardless of its origin, *The Marines' Hymn* has remained a revered icon of the United States Marine Corps for almost 200 years.

In 1929 *The Marines' Hymn* became the *official* hymn of the Corps. Thirteen years later in November 1942 the Commandant approved a change in the words of the first verse, fourth line. Because of the increasing use of aircraft in the Corps, the words were changed to "In the air, on land, and sea." No other changes have been made since that time. When you have attained absolute perfection, there is no need for further modification:

> From the Halls of Montezuma,
> > To the Shores of Tripoli;
> We fight our country's battles
> > In the air, on land, and sea;
> First to fight for right and freedom
> > And to keep our honor clean;
> We are proud to claim the title
> > Of UNITED STATES MARINES.

> Our flag's unfurled to every breeze,
> > From dawn to setting sun;
> We have fought in every clime and place
> > Where we could take a gun;
> In the snow of far off northern lands
> > And in sunny tropic scenes;
> You will find us always on the job --
> > The UNITED STATES MARINES.

> Here's health to you and to our Corps,
>   Which we are proud to serve;
> In many a strife we've fought for life
>   And never lost our nerve;
> If the Army and the Navy
>   Ever look on Heaven's scenes;
> They will find the streets are guarded
>   By UNITED STATES MARINES.

Sir Winston Churchill, British Prime Minister, became an ardent admirer of the U.S. Marine Corps. In the company of guests of state, he often demonstrated his respect for U.S. Marines by reciting, from memory, all three verses of *The Marines' Hymn.*

Battle Colors of the Marine Corps: Two hundred years ago there were no radios. Combat communications, out of yelling range, posed a big problem. In a large assault, or defense, troops relied on visual signals. Usually they would "follow their colors." They followed the flag of their military unit.

During their first hundred-plus years, U.S. Marines carried a variety of flags, or *battle colors*, in combat. The Marine who carried the colors, or standard, had great responsibility and was accorded great honor. Of course, all combatants, good guys and bad guys alike, had this communication scheme figured out: a no-brainer. Everyone always targeted the enemy color-bearer, just as the combatants of today always target the enemy radioman. Neither color-bearers of old, nor modern combatants sporting long whip antennas, could count on surviving a pitched battle.

Technology evolved over time. Around 1900, field telephones, followed by radios, became a better way to communicate on the field of battle. Nonetheless, tradition mandated that the battle colors of military units be afforded a place of honor. On 18 January 1939, gold and scarlet were incorporated into today's Marine Corps flag, the *Battle Colors of the Marine Corps.*

The 50 colored streamers which adorn the Battle Colors represent the battle accomplishments of the Corps, awarded by both the United States and foreign governments. The Marine Barracks in

Washington, DC, retains the official Battle Colors. A duplicate is maintained in the office of the Commandant in the Pentagon.

Blood Stripe: The revered "Blood Stripe" is the scarlet piping on the trousers of Dress Blues uniforms worn by Marine Corps officers and NCOs. Look at the history books! That piping is there for a *reason*, not simply for aesthetic purposes.

The United States and Mexico fought what Americans call the Mexican War. The U.S. Navy ships and their Marines played a dramatic role. But a single battalion of Marines accompanying Gen. Winfield Scott's Army would garner the glory. They would give the Corps *"the halls of Montezuma."*

Gen. Scott's Army prepared to lay siege to Mexico City on 12 September 1847. But first Gen. Scott had to neutralize lofty Chapultepec Castle, the Mexican strongpoint that was the key to defense of the city. Before the Spanish conquest centuries earlier, the castle had been the home of Montezuma II, the great Aztec Empire monarch. Now it bristled with guns and defenders. The castle, with its massive high walls, sat atop a volcanic rock hill. Around the base of the hill was a 15 foot wall. Beyond that wall was the steep uphill approach -- a killing ground -- to the high walls of the Chapultepec Castle fortress.

Gen. Scott's artillery belched flame, smoke, and hot steel on the morning of 12 September. All day American cannon poured shot and canister at the fortress. The firestorm had no appreciable effect; the Mexican defenders stayed put behind their walls, secure and confident. The next day the American artillery resumed the bombardment. Still, there was no tangible result.

In desperation, Gen. Scott called upon the battalion of Marines. The audacious Marines poured over the first wall and climbed the hill toward the castle. Protected behind their breastworks, the Mexicans fired down at the Marine attackers as they clawed their way up the hill. The volcanic slope turned into a charnel house. The blood of the dead and wounded could not soak into the rock. One first-hand account of the battle noted: "The rock terraces of Chapultepec literally ran with blood."

Yet, the Marines would not be denied. They reached the castle wall, battered down the gate of the citadel, and charged inside.

Although met with a whirlwind of fire, they routed the Mexican infantry defenders. Then the Marines shot down the mounted Mexican lancers who staged a ferocious counterattack. The victorious Marine Warriors who had survived then raised the American flag over Montezuma's ancient fortress.

Chapultepec Castle! The Marines won the victory and the glory, but the high price of that victory was paid in blood.

Today, U.S. Marines sew the Blood Stripe onto the trousers of their Dress Blues when they attain the rank of corporal. They wear this scarlet piping in honor of their Marine brothers whose blood was shed during the bitter battle for *"the halls of Montezuma."*

Marine Corps Band: The armies of the ancient Greeks and Romans knew their stuff. Their military drummers dictated cadence and -- maybe -- confidence as their legions marched into combat. By the 1700s in Europe and America, fifers added "fighting spirit" as they accompanied the military drummers.

The U.S. Marine Corps drummers and fifers evolved into the U.S. Marine Corps Band, the oldest musical organization in the United States. On 11 July 1798 the U.S. President, John Adams, signed a congressional act that formalized the band members as "a drum major, a fife major, and thirty-two drums and fifes." There was no war at the time, so the band concentrated on its music. The Marine Band held its first known concert in Washington on 21 August 1800. By December of that year the inventory of instruments had expanded to include two oboes, two clarinets, two French horns, and a bassoon. During the presidency of Thomas Jefferson, he declared the new Marine Band to be "The President's Own," a term that has survived for two centuries.

The Marine Band performs at all Presidential Inaugurations and at numerous ceremonial functions of State at the White House and elsewhere. During the summer months it entertains weekly at the famed Sunset Parade at the Marine Barracks in Washington, and on the steps of the Capitol Building. When on tour the band performs throughout the United States. John Philip Sousa, the most famous Bandmaster, composed *Semper Fidelis*, later adopted as the official musical march of the U.S. Marine Corps. Ooo-rah!

Musicians are currently selected through an audition process similar to that of major symphony orchestras. Those selected must also pass a physical examination -- it is *still* the Marine Corps, troops! Successful applicants enlist for four years "for duty with the U.S. Marine Band only," and there is no boot camp. Further, each new band member is immediately appointed to the rank of Staff Sergeant. What a deal! Historically, more than 90 percent of Marine Band members serve for 20 years or more.

The Ultimate Marine Warrior, "Chesty": All U.S. Marines know the tribute: "Goodnight, Chesty, wherever you are!" For outsiders, here is a look at the most decorated, most revered, most colorful Marine in history.

In the Marine Corps, Lewis B. "Chesty" Puller rose from Private to Lieutenant General. He devoted 37 years of his life to the Corps. Twenty-seven of those years he spent on overseas duty, most of it in combat. Chesty became a Marine living legend, the warrior who really loved to fight. There will likely never be another like him. *Time Magazine* once explained:

He shouted battle orders in a bellow that rattled the Halls of Montezuma. He stalked about under enemy fire as though he were daring anyone to hit him. He had an abiding love for the enlisted men who did the killing and dying . . . He thrived on combat until he became a legend to his troops, a born leader who went off to battle with his green eyes gleaming malevolently, a stubby pipe clenched in his crooked mouth, and a copy of Caesar's *Gallic Wars* tucked into his duffel bag.

Chesty left Virginia Military Institute and enlisted in the Corps in 1918. He was 20 years old. Within months he found himself in Haiti fighting the bandits, the Caco rebels. That fight would last five long years. Commissioned in 1924, he returned to what he loved, fighting bandits -- this time in Nicaragua.

During the 1930s Chesty commanded the famous "Horse Marines" in China, serving at Peking and Shanghai. Next came the first American offensive of World War II in the Pacific, the assault on Guadalcanal. As usual, Chesty managed to get in the thick of the fight. After that brutal struggle, he and his Marines island-hopped across the Pacific toward Japan.

When the Marines stormed the seawall at Inchon in 1950, Chesty was among them. Months later he led his beloved First Marine Regiment at the Frozen Chosin, forever carving his place in the annals of Marine Corps lore. Declining health later forced his retirement. Yet, the old warhorse did not think he was finished. At age 68 in 1966, he requested reassignment to active duty. He wanted no paper-pushing staff pogue job. He wanted a combat command. Chesty wanted to lead Marines in battle in Vietnam. Alas! The Marine Corps declined his request because of his age.

Chesty Puller departed this earthly life in 1971. Yet, he still remains the most outspoken, the most colorful, the most decorated, and the most revered Marine Warrior in the history of the U.S. Marine Corps. No one can match his charisma and love of battle. His military decorations, beginning with his *five* Navy Cross awards, are listed below:

1. Navy Cross, with four stars
2. Distinguished Service Cross (from the U.S. Army)
3. Silver Star
4. Legion of Merit, with one star and the "V" device
5. Bronze Star, with the "V" device
6. Air Medal, with two stars
7. Purple Heart
8. Presidential Unit Citation, with five stars
9. Good Conduct Medal, with one star
10. World War I Victory Medal, with one star
11. Haitian Campaign Medal
12. Nicaraguan Campaign Medal
13. Marine Corps Expeditionary Medal, with one star
14. China Service Medal
15. American Defense Medal, with one star
16. American Campaign Medal
17. Asiatic-Pacific Campaign Medal, with four stars
18. World War II Victory Medal
19. National Defense Service Medal
20. United Nations Service Medal
21. *Medaille Militaire* (Haiti)
22. *Medalla de Merito con estrella* (Nicaragua)

23. Presidential Unit Citation (Korea)
24. Ulghi Medal with Palm (Korea)
25. Cloud and Banner (China)

The ultimate Marine Warrior: LtGen. Lewis B. "Chesty" Puller, USMC. He was born on 26 June 1898; he crossed to the *other side* on 11 October 1971. Goodnight, Chesty, wherever you are!

Marine Corps War Memorial: Rising from *hallowed ground*, the Marine Corps War Memorial overlooks the Potomac River in Arlington, Virginia. Standing adjacent to Arlington National Cemetery, it is the largest bronze monument in the world. Arguably, it is also the most famous monument in the world.

A brief historical review: In the closing years of World War II, U.S. Marines fought and bled their way across the Pacific Ocean toward Japan. The Japanese knew their tiny volcanic island, Iwo Jima, would be attacked. Its crucial airfields lay only 650 miles from Tokyo, just over two hours flying time. Therefore, under the command of LtGen. Tadamichi Kuribayashi, Japan's best and brightest mining engineers turned remote Iwo Jima into a seemingly impregnable fortress.

In the volcanic rock, Korean slave laborers blasted out 16 miles of tunnels that connected 1500 rooms. Japanese engineers built underground hospitals and supply rooms under hundreds of feet of solid impenetrable rock. The rooms and tunnels linked over a thousand fortified artillery and antiaircraft batteries, plus machinegun and mortar bunkers. *Impregnable*, they believed.

Preliminary bombardment by the 16-inch guns of U.S. Navy battleships had a negligible effect on the volcanic rock fortress. Nonetheless, on 19 February 1945 the Marines stormed the beach.

Many Marines never even made it to the shore. From hundreds of fortifications, many atop 550-foot high Mount Suribachi, the Japanese rained a hail of rockets, artillery, mortar, and automatic weapons fire down upon the attacking Marines.

For both the Japanese and the Marines, the island became a charnel house. Yet, on the fourth day of the battle the Marines of 3rd Platoon, Echo Company, 2nd Battalion, 28th Marines, fought their way to the summit of Mount Suribachi. Here they raised a small American flag.

The Marines soon got a much larger flag, one that could be seen all over the island, where the battle still raged. Five Marines and a Navy corpsman mounted the new flag on a section of pipe. Together, they raised this flag atop the former Japanese bastion. The six flag-raisers represented a cross-section of America:

- PFC Ira Hayes, a full-blooded Pima Indian from Arizona.
- Sgt. Michael Strank, a Pennsylvania coal mine worker.
- Cpl. Harlon Block, a draftee from the Texas oil fields.
- PFC Franklin Sousley, a 19 year old Kentucky farm boy.
- PFC Rene Gagnon, a New Englander rejected by the Navy.
- PM2 (corpsman) John Bradley, a funeral director's apprentice.

Joe Rosenthal, of the Associated Press, photographed the men as they raised the flag. That picture, stopping time for 1/400th of a second, would become the most famous photograph of all time.

After 36 terrible days, Iwo Jima finally fell to the Marines. Of the *forty men* in 3rd Platoon who stormed the beach, *only four* escaped being killed or seriously wounded on Iwo Jima. Of the six men who raised the flag, Cpl. Block, Sgt. Strank, and PFC Sousley were killed-in-action within days. They are among the 6,821 Americans who never left Iwo Jima alive. Further, an *additional* 19,217 Americans were maimed or grievously wounded.

In July 1947 the U.S. Congress authorized a Marine Corps War Memorial, based on the timeless photograph by Joe Rosenthal. The new memorial was sculpted by Felix de Weldon. In 108 separate pieces, it was cast in a New York foundry and then trucked south to the memorial site. Ground-breaking and assembly began on 19 February 1954, the ninth anniversary of the Iwo Jima landing. The final cost of $850,000 was borne entirely by donations, 96 percent of them from Marine Warriors.

Burnished into the base of polished black Swedish granite, in gold letters, is the inscription, "Uncommon Valor Was A Common Virtue." On the opposite side is the additional inscription:

In Honor And Memory Of The Men Of The United States Marine Corps Who Have Given Their Lives To Their Country Since 10 November 1775

Inscribed in gold are the names of the campaigns in which Marines have fought since 1775. Dwight D. Eisenhower, U.S. President, delivered the dedication address on 10 November 1954, the 179th birthday of the Corps.

From the memorial, sometimes called the Iwo Jima Memorial, visitors can look across the Potomac River to the Mall in Washington. The Lincoln Memorial, the Washington Monument, and the U.S. Capitol building are visible, all in a row.

At the Marine Corps War Memorial the five Marines and their corpsman are forever immortalized in bronze. Night and day, 365 days per year, they raise the American flag for Corps and Country.

The Marine Corps War Memorial honors the *supreme sacrifice* of all Marines who have fallen in battle in the service of their country. Here, they never grow old. Here, they live eternally. Here, they live on *hallowed ground.* Never forget.

Women Marines: The Marines are looking for *A Few Good Men.* They keep their eyes peeled for *A Few Good Women,* too.

In secret, Lucy Brewer became the first woman to serve in the Marine Corps. Disguised as a gung-ho man (a pretty nifty trick, aboard ship), she served as a member of the Marine Detachment aboard the *USS Constitution* during the War of 1812.

Over 100 years later on 12 August 1918, the Secretary of the Navy granted authority to enroll women for clerical duty in the Marine Corps Reserve. The next day, Opha M. Johnson enlisted and became the first *official* Woman Marine. During the remainder of World War I, 305 women enlisted to "free a man to fight."

Over 20 years later during World War II, roughly 1000 officers and 18,000 enlisted women served, led by Col. Ruth C. Streeter. During the last year of the war, most male Marines were battling the Japanese in the Pacific. In their absence, Women Marines constituted over half of the personnel at Marine Corps bases in the continental United States.

A year after the end of the war, the Marine Corps retained a small nucleus of Women Marines in a postwar reserve. Then in 1948, Congress passed the Women's Armed Forces Integration Act. It authorized women in the regular component of the Corps. At the time, women could not constitute over two percent of the total force. Also, they could not hold *permanent* rank above lieutenant colonel. The Corps appointed Katherine A. Towle as the Director of Women Marines; she held the *temporary* rank of colonel. The following year the Marine Corps set up a recruit training battalion for women recruits at Parris Island, and a women's officer training class at Quantico.

During the Vietnam War in March 1967, gungy MSgt. Barbara Dulinsky requested reassignment from the United States to Vietnam. The Marine Corps transferred her to the main military headquarters (MACV) in Saigon. There, MSgt. Dulinsky became the first Woman Marine to be stationed in a war-torn country.

Seven years later the Commandant authorized Women Marines to serve with *specialized rear echelon* elements of the Fleet Marine Force. Still, these women were prohibited from deployment with combat units, or units which could conceivably be engaged in combat. Women were specifically banned from infantry, artillery, and armor units. Further, they could not serve on aircrews.

In May 1978, BGen. Margaret Brewer became the first general grade Woman Marine, serving as Director of Information. Twenty-two years later roughly 1000 Women Marines deployed to Southwest Asia prior to and during the Gulf War. Later, because of legal mandates, the Corps accepted women into Naval Aviation pilot training. In July 1993, 2ndLt. Sarah Deal became the first such Woman Marine to begin training. She graduated and received her Golden Wings on 21 April 1995.

The next year MGen. Carol A. Mutter became the first two-star Woman Marine. Two years later she got promoted again, the first Woman Marine to wear three stars. By the turn of the century in the year 2000, over 700 Women Marines comprised about four percent of the officer corps. Plus, over 8000 Women Marines made up roughly five percent of the active enlisted force.

The elite combat-oriented Marine Corps remains the only U.S. armed service with the wisdom and courage to maintain separate basic training units for men and women. Despite the childish whining of liberal theorists, despite the rabid ranting of ignorant "politically correct" zealots, the Marine Corps has not faltered. Basic training for men and women will remain separate -- but equal. All who qualify *earn the title*, United States Marine.

Mission of the Marine Corps: Watch your back! Over the years there have been many efforts to abolish the Marine Corps. It is noteworthy, however, that none of these efforts ever came in wartime. But in time of peace, "how quickly they forget."

The last major effort to eliminate the Marine Corps came in the late 1940s. During World War II the American military had prevented a worldwide return to the Dark Ages. But after the war by the hundreds of thousands, soldiers, sailors, and Marines were discharged and returned to civilian life. Within two years only a skeletal United States military force remained.

Tens of thousands of military aircraft, tanks, ships, and other tools of war headed for the scrap heap. And with world peace supposedly assured, why keep the Marine Corps? Many believed that despite the exemplary combat performance of the Marines during the war, the Corps had no relevant post-war role. After all, the United States had *the bomb*. Only the United States had harnessed the power of the atom, the power that had ended the war by bringing Japan to its knees. Surely any future war could be won, or prevented, by the United States and its awesome atomic bombs. Land forces seemed almost irrelevant.

Harry S. Truman, U.S. President, led the drive to disband the Corps. All remaining Marines could be absorbed into the Army or discharged, he openly advocated.

However, the wise heads in Congress prevailed. They reasoned that as long as America needed defending, America needed its Marine Corps. To thwart other attempts to abolish the Marines, Congress codified the mission and role of the Corps. There would be a minimum of "three combat divisions and three air wings" within the Corps. Congress spelled out the role of the U.S. Marine Corps in the National Security Act of 1947, as amended:

The Marine Corps, within the Department of the Navy, shall be so organized as to include not less than three combat divisions and three air wings, and such other land combat, aviation, and other services as may be organic therein. The Marine Corps shall be organized, trained, and equipped to provide fleet marine forces of combined arms, together with supporting air components, for service with the fleet in the seizure or defense of advanced naval bases and for the conduct of such land operations as may be essential to the prosecution of a naval campaign. In addition the Marine Corps shall provide detachments and organizations for service on armed vessels of the Navy, shall provide security detachments for the protection of naval property at naval stations and bases, and shall perform such other duties as the President may direct. However these additional duties may not detract from or interfere with the operations for which the Marine Corps is primarily organized.

Commandants of the Marine Corps: Since its birth in 1775 the Marine Corps has been led by 33 different men. The first of these Marine leaders, Samuel Nicholas, *technically* never held the title of Commandant. His commission as "Captain of Marines," signed by John Hancock, begins as follows:

IN CONGRESS. The Delegates of the United Colonies of New-Hampshire, Massachusetts Bay, Rhode-Island, Connecticut, New-York, New-Jersey, Pennsylvania, the Counties of New-Castle, Kent, and Suffex on Delaware, Maryland, Virginia, North-Carolina, South-Carolina, and Georgia, to **Samuel Nicholas Esquire**. We, reposing especial Trust and Confidence in your Patriotism, Valour, Conduct and Fidelity, Do by these Presents, constitute and appoint you to be **Captain of Marines** in the service of the Thirteen United Colonies of North-America, fitted out for the defense of American Liberty . . . .

The term "Commandant" did not come into use for over a quarter-century. Notwithstanding this technicality, Samuel Nicholas is considered the first of the lineage, the first Commandant. These 33 United States Marine Corps leaders are listed below:

1. Samuel Nicholas 1775-1781
2. William W. Burrows 1798-1804
3. Franklin Wharton 1804-1818
4. Anthony Gale 1819-1820
5. Archibald Henderson 1820-1859
6. John Harris 1859-1864

7. Jacob Zeilin 1864-1876
8. Charles G. McCawley 1876-1891
9. Charles Heywood 1891-1903
10. George F. Elliott 1903-1910
11. William P. Biddle 1911-1914
12. George Barnett 1914-1920
13. John A. Lejeune 1920-1929
14. Wendell C. Neville 1929-1930
15. Ben H. Fuller 1930-1934
16. John H. Russell Jr. 1934-1936
17. Thomas Holcomb 1936-1943
18. Alexander A. Vandegrift 1944-1947
19. Clifton B. Cates 1948-1951
20. Lemuel C. Shepherd Jr. 1952-1955
21. Randolph M. Pate 1956-1959
22. David M. Shoup 1960-1963
23. Wallace M. Greene Jr. 1964-1967
24. Leonard F. Chapman Jr. 1968-1971
25. Robert E. Cushman Jr. 1972-1975
26. Louis H. Wilson Jr. 1975-1979
27. Robert H. Barrow 1979-1983
28. Paul X. Kelley 1983-1987
29. Alfred M. Gray Jr. 1987-1991
30. Carl E. Mundy Jr. 1991-1995
31. Charles C. Krulak 1995-1999
32. James L. Jones Jr. 1999-2003
33. Michael W. Hagee 2003--

Note: On 16 March 1861 the Congress of the Confederate States of America established the *Confederate States Marine Corps*. On 23 May 1861, Col. Lloyd J. Beall (a West Point graduate who resigned his U.S. Army commission to "go south") was appointed as *Colonel-Commandant*, CSMC. Col. Beall served as Colonel-Commandant of the C.S. Marine Corps until the end of the American Civil War in 1865.

Sergeants Major of the Marine Corps: The rank of Sergeant Major dates back to the British Army in the sixteenth century. The first U.S. Marine to attain the rank of Sergeant Major was Archibald Summers in 1801. As the years passed more Marines attained this highest enlisted rank in the Corps.

In 1957 the Commandant, Gen. Randolph M. Pate, created a new title, *Sergeant Major of the Marine Corps*. This was not a new rank. Instead, it was a new title for a new office. This new title would be bestowed upon only one Marine. He would serve as the *enlisted man's general*, so to speak.

Gen. Pate appointed Wilbur Bestwick as the first Marine to hold the new title and office. Over the years, 14 more men have followed in SgtMaj. Bestwick's steps. Their office in the Pentagon is roughly 50 feet from the office of the Commandant. The Sergeant Major of the Marine Corps meets regularly with generals of the Marine Corps and other services. His input and his recommendations carry great weight.

The names of the 15 Marines who have held the title, Sergeant Major of the Marine Corps, are listed below:

1. Wilbur Bestwick 1957-1959
2. Francis D. Rauber 1959-1962
3. Thomas J. McHugh 1962-1965
4. Herbert J. Sweet 1965-1969
5. Joseph W. Dailey 1969-1973
6. Clinton A. Puckett 1973-1975
7. Henry H. Black 1975-1977
8. John E. Massaro 1977-1979
9. LeLand D. Crawford 1979-1983
10. Robert E. Cleary 1983-1987
11. David W. Sommers 1987-1991
12. Harold G. Overstreet 1991-1995
13. Lewis G. Lee 1995-1999
14. Alford L. McMichael 1999-2003
15. John L. Estrada 2003--

Note: On 16 March 1861 the Congress of the Confederate States of America established the *Confederate States Marine Corps*. Almost three years later on 1 February 1864, Edwin Wallace was appointed as *Sergeant Major of the Confederate States Marine Corps*. Wallace (a former Royal Marine, educated at the Duke of

York military school in London, and the son of a Sergeant Major in the Royal Marines) was the only man who served as Sergeant Major of the C.S. Marine Corps.

Confederate States Marine Corps: Eighty-five years after the birth of the United States, civil war ripped the nation apart. Eleven southern states, stymied by political mandates and economic sanctions, seceded from the union. The new Confederate States of America set up a provisional government at Montgomery, Alabama (later relocated to Richmond, Virginia), in February 1861.

Included in the C.S. Congress mandates was a Confederate States Marine Corps. The Confederacy patterned its new Corps of Marines after the time-tested U.S. Marine Corps. For fighting men in its new Corps, the new C.S. Congress approved a battalion of C.S. Marines in March 1861.

C.S. Marine Corps recruiting posed no problem. Many United States military men had elected to "go south" with their home states. The Army, Navy, and Marine Corps of the Confederacy quickly welcomed these military veterans.

Under their Commandant, Col. Lloyd J. Beall, the C.S. Marines began their primary duty, service aboard C.S. Navy warships. When the first Confederate commerce raider sallied forth from New Orleans and headed for the Atlantic Ocean, she carried a detachment of 20 C.S. Marines. The shipboard role of these Confederate "soldiers of the sea" remained identical to that of their U.S. Marine counterparts.

Throughout the war in the beleaguered Confederate Navy, the C.S. Marines served with distinction. For example, while the commerce raider *CSS Sumter* was laid up at Gibraltar, its Acting Master's Mate murdered the Commanding Officer in October 1862. The senior Marine aboard, Cpl. George Stephenson, took charge (as Marines traditionally do). After restoring order, he reported the murder to Confederate Naval Authorities in London. Because of his initiative and military bearing, Cpl. Stephenson was ordered to take command of the warship. This gung-ho Marine corporal, later promoted to sergeant, became the new Commanding Officer of the *CSS Sumter* (he survived the war).

C.S. Marines served aboard almost all of the Confederate Navy river vessels.   They also manned the seagoing men-o-war and commerce raiders: *CSS Chickamauga, CSS Shenandoah, CSS Georgia, CSS Stonewall, CSS Rappahannock,* and others.   The most successful was the *CSS Alabama,* which sank or captured over $11,000,000 worth of northern shipping.   Nonetheless, the most famous was the *CSS Virginia* (formerly the *USS Merrimack*).   In the historic first battle between ironclad warships in March 1862, the *CSS Virginia* crew included its detachment of C.S. Marines.

Born in 1861, the C.S. Marine Corps would last only four years. The war left southern manufacturing capacity, originally only 11 percent that of the industrialized north, in ruins.   The anticipated support from Europe never materialized.   The agricultural base evaporated.   There was no food, no money, no infrastructure, no way to break the strangling naval blockade, no way to resupply the troops in the field, no way to stop the invading juggernaut.

Dedication to cause, however admirable, eventually proved to be no substitute for beans and bullets.   When the war ended in 1865, the C.S. Marine Corps faded into the history books.

Marine Corps Recruiting Posters: The Continental Congress created the Continental Marines on 10 November 1775.   Robert Mullan, the first Marine Recruiter, began his search for A Few Good Men.   He used cold beer as the primary enlistment incentive.

Two months later the first "recruiting poster" (see the sub-chapter, "First Marine Corps Recruiting Poster") rolled off the press.   Over the years, recruiting efforts evolved with the changing role of the Corps.   During its first 100-plus years, Marines emphasized their primary role as naval infantry.   Later the Corps' recruiting efforts touted the combat ferocity of Marine Warriors.

Today, Marine Recruiting Posters *challenge* potential recruits. Many try to *earn the title,* to become transformed in both mind and body.   The tenacious few who succeed become an integral part of *their* legendary Corps, *their* storied Brotherhood of Marines.

Some of the Marine Corps Recruiting Posters are depicted on the following pages.   Assistance from the Marine Corps Recruiting Command is gratefully acknowledged (see page v):

U.S. MARINE CORPS

RECRUITING SERVICE.

Wanted, for the United States Marine Corps,

Able-bodied **MEN**, between the ages of 18 and 40 years, not less than 5 feet 5 inches high, and of good character.

SOLDIERS serving in this Corps perform duty at Navy Yards and on board United States Ships of War on Foreign Stations. which affords a splendid opportunity to travel and see the world.

The term of service is **FOUR YEARS**: and if a soldier re-enlists at the expiration of that time, his pay will be increased **two dollars** per month for the first re-enlistment, with a further addition of **one dollar** per month for all subsequent re-enlistments.

By good conduct and attention to duty. a soldier will certainly rise to the position of a non-commissioned officer.

SERGEANTS in the Marine Corps frequently have independent command of guards on Sloops-of-War, and always on Gunboats. The following is the rate of pay as now established:

GRADE.	PAY OF UNITED STATES MARINE CORPS.		
	Pay per Month.	Pay per Annum.	Pay for Four Years.
To the First or Orderly Sergeant of a Company or Guard, - - - - - - - - -	$24 00	$288 00	$1.152 00
All other Sergeants, each. - - - - - -	20 00	240 00	960 00
Corporals, - - - - - - - - - - - -	18 00	216 00	864 00
Musicians, - - - - - - - - - - - -	16 00	192 00	768 00
Privates, - - - - - - - - - - - -	16 00	192 00	768 00
At Sea, the extra pay is - - - - - -	1 50	18 00	72 00

In addition to the pay as above stated, one ration per day and an abundant supply of the best clothing is allowed to every soldier. A soldier who is careful of his clothing can save during his enlistment from 50 to 80 dollars. Quarters, fuel, and medical attendance are always provided by the Government, without deduction from the soldier's pay. If a soldier should become disabled in the line of his duties, the law provides for him a Pension.

All other information which may be desired, will be given at the Rendezvous.

LIEUT. H. C. COCHRANE,

Recruiting Officer.

RECRUITING RENDEZVOUS,

PARDEE'S BUILDING, CHICAGO. May, 1866.

USMC Recruiting Poster, May 1866.

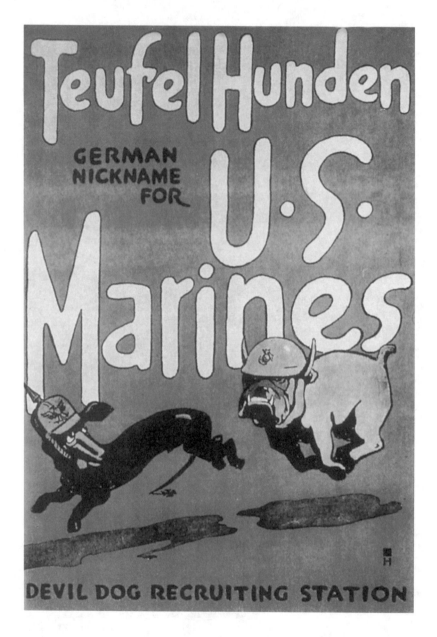

USMC Recruiting Poster, c 1918.   During the bloody fighting in
France in 1918, official German dispatches repeatedly called the
attacking U.S. Marines "Teufel Hunden," which means, *Devil Dogs*.
The term gained widespread popularity in the U.S. media. It also
found its way onto Marine Corps Recruiting Posters.

Only a few good men and women can become Marines. Those who understand the importance of discipline and dedication. Those who want to further the ideals that have enabled the Marines to defend American interests at home and around the world for more than two centuries. Only individuals who have the self-discipline, pride and self-respect that we seek can become one of The Few; The Proud; The Marines.

USMC Recruiting Booklet content, c 2000. On 20 March 1779, Capt. William Jones, Continental Marines, placed an advertisement in *The Providence Gazette*. He asked for "a few good men" to enlist in the Corps for duty on Continental Navy ships. Jones knew "a few" would be enough: The Few; The Proud; The Marines.

Life in the Marine Corps

Marine Corps Birthday: All U.S. Marines are gung-ho. But few can match the vision, tenacity, and commitment of the famous thirteenth Commandant, the fighting LtGen. John A. Lejeune. In 1921 he issued Marine Corps Order No. 47.

Gen. Lejeune's order summarized the history, mission, and traditions of the U.S. Marine Corps. It further directed that this *Birthday Message* (see the next sub-chapter) be read to all Marines throughout the world each year on 10 November. This annual event would honor the founding of the Corps on that day in 1775.

Many U.S. Marine commands began to not only honor the birthday, but *celebrate* it. In 1923 the Marine Barracks at Ft. Mifflin, Pennsylvania, staged a formal dance. The Marines at the Washington Navy Yard arranged a mock battle on the parade ground. At Quantanamo Bay, Cuba, the Marine baseball team played a Cuban team and won, 9 to 8.

The first "formal" Birthday Ball took place in Philadelphia in 1925. First class Marine Corps style, all the way! Guests included the Commandant, the Secretary of War (in 1925 the term "politically correct" did not exist; it was Secretary of *War*, not Secretary of *Defense*), and a host of statesmen and elected officials. Prior to the Ball, Gen. Lejeune unveiled a memorial plaque at Tun Tavern. Then the entourage headed for the Benjamin Franklin Hotel and an evening of festivities and frolicking.

Over the years the annual Birthday Ball grew and grew, taking on a life of its own. In 1952 the Commandant, Gen. Lemuel C. Shepherd Jr., formalized the cake-cutting ceremony and other traditional observances. For example, Marine Corps policy now mandates that the first piece of cake be presented to the oldest U.S. Marine present. The second piece goes to the youngest Marine. Among the many such mandates is a solemn reading of the Commandant's annual birthday message to the Corps.

Like the U.S. Marine Corps itself, the annual Birthday Ball has evolved from simple origins into the polished and professional ceremony of today. Nonetheless, one thing remains constant: the tenth day of November! This unique holiday for Marine Warriors is a day of camaraderie, a day of pride, a day to honor Corps and Country. Throughout the world on 10 November, U.S. Marines celebrate the birth of their Corps -- the most loyal, most feared, most revered, most lethal, and most professional fighting machine the world has ever known.

Postscript: Some sources in-the-know have *claimed* that after the annual Birthday Ball, some Marine Warriors need to "stand down" for a day and recuperate. Maybe. Maybe not. In either event, the U.S. Congress has eliminated any potential problem.

Since the flower-power days of the 1960s, Veterans Day had been observed on the fourth Monday in October. But in 1978, Congress restored *11 November* as the day on which all Americans observe Veterans Day. Consequently, *if* any Marine Warriors need to "stand down" the day after their birthday celebration, the U.S. Congress has given them a *national holiday* on which to do so.

First Marine Corps Birthday Message: The annual Marine Corps Birthday is more than a celebration each year. It is a time for each U.S. Marine to reflect upon the legacy of his Corps and upon the awesome responsibilities lying ahead.

LtGen. John A. Lejeune initiated the annual observance. His original birthday message to his Corps, penned in 1921, still stands as a monument to the Brotherhood of Marines:

> On November 10, 1775, a Corps of Marines was created by a resolution of the Continental Congress. Since that date, many thousand men have borne the name, Marine. In memory of them, it is fitting that we who are Marines should commemorate the Birthday of our Corps by calling to mind the glories of its long and illustrious history.
>
> The record of our Corps is one which will bear comparison with that of the most famous military organizations in the world's history. During 90 of the 146 years of its existence the Marine Corps has been in action against the nation's foes. From the battle of Trenton to the Argonne, Marines have won foremost honors in war, and in the long eras of tranquility at

home. Generation after generation of Marines have grown gray in war in both hemispheres, and in every corner of the seven seas, so that our country and its citizens might enjoy peace and security.

In every battle and skirmish since the birth of our Corps, Marines have acquitted themselves with the greatest distinction, winning new honors on each occasion until the term "Marine" has come to signify all that is highest in military efficiency and soldierly virtue.

This high name of distinction and soldierly repute we who are Marines today have received from those who preceded us in the Corps. With it we also received from them the eternal spirit which has animated our Corps from generation to generation and has been the distinguishing mark of Marines in every age. So long as that spirit continues to flourish, Marines will be found equal to every emergency in the future as they have been in the past, and the men of our nation will regard us as worthy successors to the long line of illustrious men who have served as "Soldiers of the Sea" since the founding of the Corps.

Marine Corps Motto: The Marine Corps adopted *Semper Fidelis* as its official motto in 1883 (*Semper Fidelis* is also the title of the official musical March of the Marine Corps). Translated from Latin, Semper Fidelis means "Always Faithful." U.S. Marines use an abbreviated verbal version, "Semper Fi," to voice loyalty and commitment to their Marine brothers-in-arms.

Previous mottos of the Marine Corps were (1) *To the Shores of Tripoli*, adopted in 1805; (2) *Fortitude*, adopted in 1812; (3) *From the Halls of Montezuma to the Shores of Tripoli*, adopted in 1848; and (4) *By Sea and by Land*, adopted in the 1850s.

Marine Corps Mascot: Thanks to the German Army, the U.S. Marine Corps has an *unofficial* mascot.

During World War I, many official German reports had called the attacking Marines "teufel-hunden," meaning *Devil Dogs*. These beasts were the ferocious mountain dogs of Bavarian folklore.

Soon afterward a U.S. Marine Recruiting Poster depicted a snarling English Bulldog wearing a Marine Corps helmet (see the sub-chapter, "Marine Corps Recruiting Posters"). Because of the tenacity and demeanor of the breed, the image took root with both the Marines and the public. The Marines soon unofficially adopted the English Bulldog as their mascot.

At their base at Quantico, Virginia, Marines obtained a registered English Bulldog, *King Bulwark*. In a formal ceremony on 14 October 1922, BGen. Smedley D. Butler signed documents which enlisted the bulldog, renamed *Jiggs*, for the "term of life." Pvt. Jiggs got an official USMC waiver and avoided boot camp. He immediately began his inspirational duties in the Corps.

A gungy hard-charging canine Marine, Pvt. Jiggs did not remain a private for long. Within three months he sported corporal chevrons on his custom-made uniform. On New Years Day in 1924, Cpl. Jiggs got promoted to sergeant. And in a meteoric rise he got promoted again -- this time, all the way to sergeant major -- seven months later.

SgtMaj. Jiggs' death on 9 January 1927 was mourned throughout the Corps. The four-footed USMC sergeant major, in a miniature satin-lined coffin, lay in state in a hangar at Quantico. Row upon row of floral sprays from non-canine admirers flanked the coffin. Amid much pomp and ceremony, the Corps interred SgtMaj. Jiggs with full military honors.

A replacement mascot was soon on the way to Quantico. Former heavyweight boxing champion James J. "Gene" Tunney, a Marine veteran who had fought with the Corps in France, donated his English Bulldog. Renamed *Jiggs II*, the new mascot stepped into the role of his predecessor.

Big problem! No discipline! Jiggs II loved to chase people, and he *bit* people, too. He showed a total lack of respect for authority. The new Jiggs would likely have made an outstanding combat Marine, but barracks life did not suit him. After one of his many rampages he died of heat exhaustion in 1928.

Nonetheless, other bulldogs followed. During the 1930s, 1940s, and early 1950s they all were named *Smedley*, a tribute to the colorful and gung-ho Gen. Butler.

In the late 1950s the Marine Barracks in Washington, the oldest post in the Corps, became the new home for the four-footed mascot. Renamed *Chesty* to honor the legendary LtGen. Lewis B. "Chesty" Puller, the mascot made his first public appearance at the Evening Parade on 5 July 1957. In his sporty canine Dress Blues, Chesty became an immediate media darling, a smash hit!

After the demise of the original Chesty, the replacement was named Chesty II. Unfortunately he turned into an uncontrollable undisciplined renegade. You name it, he did it. Chesty II even escaped and went AWOL once; two days later the Washington police returned him in their paddy wagon. About the only thing Chesty II ever managed to do correctly was to sire a replacement.

In contrast to his father, Chesty III proved to be a model Marine. The Evening Parade crowds loved him. He even became a favorite of neighborhood children, for which he was meritoriously awarded a Good Conduct Medal.

Other bulldogs followed Chesty III (bulldogs do not live long). When Chesty VI died after an Evening Parade, a Marine detachment in Tennessee called Washington. Their local bulldog mascot, LCpl. Bodacious Little, was standing by for PCS orders to Washington, they reported.

Upon arrival at the Marine Barracks in Washington, LCpl. Little got ceremoniously renamed Chesty VII. He and the English Bulldogs who followed him reflected the fighting spirit of the U.S. Marines. Tough, muscular, aggressive, fearless, and often arrogant, they are the ultimate canine warriors.

English Bulldogs! Teufel-hunden! Devil Dogs! They epitomize the ethos of the Warrior Culture of the U.S. Marines.

Corps Values: Why are U.S. Marines considered the world's premier warriors? What traits place Marine Warriors above the wannabes? Other military services have rigorous training and weapons of equal or greater lethality. Why do U.S. Marines stand head and shoulders above the crowd?

The truth lies in the individual Marine. He did not *join* the Marines. Roughly 40,000 try each year. Those who survive the crucible of Marine basic training have been sculpted in mind and body. They have *become* Marines.

Once he has *earned the title* and entered the Brotherhood of Marines, a new warrior must draw upon the legacy of his Corps.

Therein lies his strength. In return, the strength of the Corps lies in the individual Marine. The *character* (often defined as "what you are in the dark") of these warriors is defined by the three constant Corps Values: Honor, Courage, and Commitment.

Honor: Honor requires each Marine to exemplify the ultimate standard in ethical and moral conduct. Honor is many things; honor mandates many things. A U.S. Marine must never lie, never cheat, never steal. But that is not enough. Much more is required. Each Marine must cling to an uncompromising code of *personal integrity*, accountable for his actions and holding others accountable for theirs. And above all, honor mandates that a Marine never sully the reputation of his Corps.

Courage: Simply stated, courage is honor in action -- and more. Courage is moral strength, the will to heed the inner voice of conscience, the will to do what is right regardless of the conduct of others. It is mental discipline, an adherence to a higher standard. Courage means willingness to take a stand for what is right in spite of adverse consequences. Throughout the history of the Corps this courage has sustained Marines during the chaos, perils, and hardships of combat. And every day it enables each Marine to look in the mirror -- and smile.

Commitment: Total dedication to Corps and Country. Gung-ho Marine teamwork. All for one, one for all. By whatever name or cliche, commitment is a combination of (1) selfless determination and (2) relentless dedication to excellence. Marines never give up, never give in, never willingly accept second best. Excellence always remains the goal. When their active duty days are over, each Marine will remain a Marine reservist, retired Marine, or a Marine veteran. There is no such thing as an ex-Marine or a former-Marine. Once a Marine, always a Marine! Commitment never dies.

The three Corps Values: Honor, Courage, and Commitment. They form the bedrock of the character of each individual Marine. They are the foundation of his Corps. These three values, handed down from generation to generation, have made U.S. Marines the

Warrior Elite. The U.S. Marine Corps: the most respected, most revered, and most feared fighting machine on Earth.

Blood Chit: The document you never want to use!

Blood Chit is the common term for the written notice, in several languages, carried by Marine aircrews in combat. If their aircraft is shot down, the notice (1) identifies the Marines as Americans and (2) encourages the local population to assist them.

The concept is over 200 years old. Jean-Pierre Blanchard, the famous French balloonist, came to America in 1793 to demonstrate hot air balloon flight. He would ascend from Philadelphia. Where he would come down, of course, no one knew. Further, Blanchard did not speak English. George Washington, the U.S. President, gave Blanchard a letter addressed to "All citizens of the United States." The letter asked that Blanchard be befriended and given safe passage back to Philadelphia.

Thereafter, this idea lay dormant for over 100 years. But in World War I the British RAF issued "ransom notes" to its combat pilots flying in India and Mesopotamia. These notes, written in Arabic, Urdu, Farsi, and Pashto languages, promised a reward to anyone bringing an *unharmed* British pilot or observer to the nearest British outpost. British airmen called the notes "goolie chits" (goolie was the Hindustani word for *ball*). Many hostile tribesmen had been turning captured airmen over to local women for *castration*, so ransom notes included the word, *unharmed.*

When the mercenary Flying Tigers went to China in 1937 to battle the Japanese, they carried "blood chits." These printed notices bore the Chinese flag and Chinese lettering which stated:

> This foreign person has come to China to help in the war effort. Soldiers and civilians, one and all, should rescue, protect, and provide him with medical care.

Later, when the United States officially entered World War II in 1941, it issued blood chits in almost 50 different languages. A reward was offered to those who assisted downed fliers.

The U.S. government kept its word. The greatest reward ever given went to the family that aided a B-29 crew shot down on 12

July 1950, two weeks after the start of the Korean War. North Korean civilians found the badly injured crewmen. Yu Ho Chun discovered the blood chit in the pocket of one flier. He gave the Americans medical aid. Then at great personal risk, he put them on a junk and sailed them 100 miles down the coast to safety. Two weeks later the North Korean Army found Chun, tortured him, and then killed him. But 43 years later in 1993, the United States paid a $100,000.00 reward to his son, Yu Song Dan.

During the war in Vietnam the fighter, attack, and helicopter crews carried new blood chits. These chits displayed the American flag, plus an appeal in 14 languages: English, Burmese, Thai, Old Chinese, New Chinese, Laotian, Cambodian, Tagalog, Vietnamese, Visayan, Malayan, French, Indonesian, and Dutch. The translation in each language was the same:

> I am a citizen of the United States of America. I do not speak your language. Misfortune forces me to seek your assistance in obtaining food, shelter, and protection. Please take me to someone who will provide for my safety and see that I am returned to my people. My government will reward you.

In Vietnam, as in World War II, some unique missions required unique measures. On certain *Black Ops* flights, in addition to their blood chits, the aircrews carried paper money and gold coins. Needless to say, these required strict inventory control. Upon return from a mission, "I lost the money!" would not suffice.

Today the United States has pre-printed blood chits for most locations throughout the world. Blood chits in the appropriate languages were issued to airmen for operations in Panama, Grenada, Somalia, Bosnia, and the wars in the Middle East. The use of blood chits will continue. The blood chit package includes money, and sometimes a pointee-talkee pictorial display.

Marine Corps Drill Instructor's Creed: Marine Corps boot camp training has always been, and must always remain, demanding. Its only two objectives are to prepare recruits for (1) the Brotherhood of Marines and (2) the hardships of combat.

On a moonlit Sunday night, 8 April 1956, a Drill Instructor at

Parris Island took his Platoon 71 on a forced march. For hours they sloshed through the muck and mire of the swamps and salt marshes surrounding the base. The Drill Instructor, a 31 year old staff sergeant, a veteran of World War II and Korea with an exemplary record, felt that his platoon needed more discipline. As he came to Ribbon Creek, the tidal stream between Horse Island and Parris Island, he shouted to his recruits:

> Anyone who can't swim will drown! Anyone who can swim will be eaten by the sharks!

The Drill Instructor plunged into the creek, dutifully followed by his platoon. All safely struggled across to the other side. After humping in circle after circle through the ever-rising water of the salt marshes, they returned to the creek. Unfortunately, by this time the tide had come in. The current was swift, and Ribbon Creek was then seven feet deep. Heavily laden by their packs and rifles, six recruits drowned in the swift dark tidal stream.

In the aftermath of the Ribbon Creek tragedy, the Marine Corps took a hard look at all aspects of recruit training and boot camp. The rigid training and ironclad discipline remained, although forced night marches through Ribbon Creek came to a screeching halt. The Parris Island Recruit Depot newspaper, *Boot*, published a new Drill Instructor's Creed on 31 August 1956:

> These are my recruits. I will train them to the best of my ability. I will develop them into smartly disciplined, physically fit, basically trained Marines, thoroughly indoctrinated in love of Corps and Country. I will demand of them, and demonstrate by my own example, the highest standards of personal conduct, morality, and professional skill.

Marine Corps Rifleman's Creed: In boot camp at Parris Island or San Diego, and in The Basic School at Quantico, no one escapes from the Rifleman's Creed. Every Marine is trained, first and foremost, as a rifleman, for it is the rifleman who must close with and destroy the enemy.

The rifleman remains the most basic tenet of Marine Corps

doctrine. All else revolves around him. Marine Aviation, Marine Armor, Marine Artillery, and all supporting arms and warfighting assets exist to support the rifleman.

MGen. William H. Rupertus, USMC, authored the Marine Corps Rifleman's Creed shortly after the Japanese attack on Pearl Harbor in 1941. The creed is commonly known as the Rifleman's Creed. It also has been called, "My Rifle: The Creed of a United States Marine." Every Marine must memorize the creed. Every Marine must live and fight by the creed:

This is my rifle. There are many like it, but this one is mine. It is my life. I must master it as I must master my life. Without me, my rifle is useless. Without my rifle, I am useless.

I must fire my rifle true. I must shoot straighter than the enemy who is trying to kill me. I must shoot him before he shoots me. I will.

My rifle and I know that what counts in war is not the rounds we fire, the noise of our burst, or the smoke we make. We know that it is the hits that count. We will hit.

My rifle is human, even as I am human, because it is my life. Thus, I will learn it as a brother. I will learn its weaknesses, its strengths, its parts, its accessories, its sights, and its barrel. I will keep my rifle clean and ready, even as I am clean and ready. We will become part of each other.

Before God I swear this creed. My rifle and I are the defenders of my country. We are the masters of our enemy. We are the saviors of my life.

So be it, until victory is America's, and there is no enemy.

Marine Corps NCO Creed: The Marine NCO, the Marine Non-Commissioned Officer, has always been the backbone of the U.S. Marine Corps. Tales of Marine NCOs and their combat exploits have become the stuff of legend. NCOs are the Corporals and Sergeants responsible for the lives of their men in combat.

Marine NCOs are leaders of warriors. They carry with them the legacy of their Corps. They uphold the unbroken traditions of honor, duty, and dedication to their Corps and Country. The NCO

Creed need not be lengthy. It is succinct and to the point:

I am a Marine NCO dedicated to training new Marines and influencing the old. I am forever conscious of each Marine under my charge, and by example will inspire him to the highest standards possible. I will strive to be patient, understanding, just, and firm. I will commend the deserving and encourage the wayward.

I will never forget that I am responsible to my Commanding Officer for the morale, discipline, and efficiency of my men. Their performance will reflect an image of me.

Marine Corps Staff NCO Creed: We all need roadmaps for life. We all need lofty goals. Those unfortunate souls who do not know what is expected of them can rarely accomplish anything of significance. They can never become a team player.

In the Marine Corps, each Marine -- regardless of rank, in war or in time of peace -- has goals and responsibilities. Goals change from time to time and from situation to situation. But the basic and constant responsibility of each Staff NCO is chiseled in stone in the Staff NCO Creed:

I am a Staff Noncommissioned Officer in the United States Marine Corps. As such, I am a member of the most unique group of professional military practitioners in the world. I am bound by duty to God, Country, and my fellow Marines to execute the demands of my position to and beyond what I believe to be the limits of my capabilities.

I realize I am the mainstay of Marine Corps discipline, and I carry myself with military grace, unbowed by the weight of command, unflinching in the execution of lawful orders, and unswerving in my dedication to the most complete success of my assigned mission.

Both my professional and personal demeanor shall be such that I may take pride if my juniors emulate me, and knowing perfection to lie beyond the grasp of any mortal hand, I shall yet strive to attain perfection that I may ever be aware of my needs and capabilities to improve myself. I shall be fair in my personal relations, just in the enforcement of discipline, true to myself and my fellow Marines, and equitable in my dealing with every man.

The Marine's Prayer: Regardless of the need, the Marine Corps has an answer for almost everything.

A one-on-one chat with The Deity is serious business. It also is an excellent idea for warriors who are expected to put their lives on the line against an assortment of formidable foes. For U.S. Marines of any faith who desire guidance when contacting their Maker, the Marine Corps has a ready aid, The Marine's Prayer:

Almighty Father, whose command is over all and whose love never fails, make me aware of Thy presence and obedient to Thy will. Keep me true to my best self, guarding me against dishonesty in purpose and deed and helping me to live so that I can face my fellow Marines, my loved ones, and Thee without shame or fear. Protect my family.

Give me the will to do the work of a Marine and to accept my share of responsibilities with vigor and enthusiasm. Grant me the courage to be proficient in my daily performance. Keep me loyal and faithful to my superiors and to the duties my Country and the Marine Corps have entrusted to me. Help me to wear my uniform with dignity, and let it remind me daily of the traditions which I must uphold.

If I am inclined to doubt, steady my faith; if I am tempted, make me strong to resist; if I should miss the mark, give me courage to try again.

Guide me with the light of truth and grant me wisdom by which I may understand the answer to my prayer.

Selected Marine Corps Slogans and Sayings: A previous sub-chapter listed some of the monikers by which Marine Warriors are known: Leatherneck, Jarhead, Gyrene, Devil Dog, etc.

In the Brotherhood of Marines, warriors use unique fighting slogans and sayings every day. Marines created some of these timeless axioms, while others originated with the media and with various admirers of the Corps:

First to Fight: The news media in the United States began using this term to describe U.S. Marines during World War I. For once, the news media was right. Marines have served in the vanguard of every American war since the founding of the Corps in 1775. They have carried out over 300 assaults on foreign shores, from the arctic to the tropics. Historically, U.S. Marines are indeed the *first to fight*.

Once a Marine, Always a Marine: This truism became the official motto of the Marine Corps League. The origin of the statement is credited to a gung-ho Marine Corps master sergeant, Paul Woyshner. During a barroom argument he shouted: "Once a Marine, always a Marine!"

MSgt. Woyshner was dead center on target. Once the title, United States Marine, has been earned, it is retained forever. The enlistment and commissioning oaths are never rescinded. Each Marine Warrior will fall into one of five categories: (1) *active duty* Marine, (2) *retired* Marine, (3) Marine *veteran*, (4) Marine *reservist*, or (5) *dead* Marine. There is no such thing as an ex-Marine or a former-Marine.

Gung-Ho: The Chinese used this term to describe Marines in China around 1900. In the Chinese language, gung-ho means *working together*. That is what the American Marines were always doing, "working together," the Chinese explained. The term stuck to Marines like glue. Today it conveys willingness to tackle any task and total commitment to the Corps.

Goodnight, Chesty, wherever you are: This is the often-used verbal tribute of respect to the late and legendary LtGen. Lewis B. "Chesty" Puller, USMC (see the sub-chapter, "The Ultimate Marine Warrior, 'Chesty'"). Without a doubt, "Chesty" was the most outspoken Marine, the most famous Marine to wear Marine Corps green. He *really loved to fight*, and he became the most decorated Marine in the history of the Corps.

Chesty enlisted as a Private. Through incredible fortitude and tenacity he evolved into a living legend. He shouted battle orders in a bellow and stalked battlefields as though impervious to enemy fire. Chesty rose to the rank of Lieutenant General. He displayed an abiding love for the Magnificent Grunts, especially the junior enlisted men who did the majority of the sacrificing and dying. He never hid his utter contempt for all staff pogues of whatever rank.

Chesty became the only Marine to be awarded the Navy Cross *five* times. The Marines' Marine! The ultimate U.S. Marine role model! "Goodnight, Chesty, wherever you are."

A Few Good Men: On 20 March 1779, Capt. William Jones, Continental Marines, advertised in *The Providence Gazette* for "a few good men" to enlist in the Corps for duty on Navy ships. The term seemed ideally suited for Marines, mainly because of the implication that "a few" good men would be enough.

This term has survived for over 200 years and has remained synonymous with Marine Warriors. Also, the phrase "A Few Good Men" makes a truly *outstanding* addition to any Marine Corps recruiting poster. ***Ooo-rah!***

Ooo-rah! The *gungy* motivational shout of the world's warrior elite. What a Marine Warrior should say (1) whenever he wants to, and (2) whenever he has already said "Semper Fi" four or more times in a row.

Sweat dries, blood clots, bones heal. Suck it up, Marine! The origin of this USMC saying has been lost in the fog of history. Yet, the meaning comes through loud and clear. Marines never give up, never give in. Marines relish challenge and adversity.

Tell it to the Marines! This familiar saying originated with the British and dates from the reign of Charles II. The U.S. Marines *borrowed* it. Then the American press began using it in reference to the Marines' gung-ho fighting esprit de corps. In popular use, it means that if you want something difficult done, or want something destroyed, "Tell it to the Marines!"

Marines go where others fear to tread: A simple statement of fact. If you have combat prowess, you can flaunt it.

Death before Dishonor: This slogan, while foreign to civilians, is a credo for Marines, a way of life. *Honor* is serious business. It is the first of the three basic Corps Values (see the sub-chapter, "Corps Values"). Also, for trivia devotees, "Death before Dishonor" is by far the most popular *tattoo* selected by U.S. Marines who elect to get a tattoo.

To Err is Human, to Forgive is Divine. Neither is Marine Corps Policy: A simple Marine Corps statement of fact. Excellence and perfection remain the standards. Had William Shakespeare lived to see this, he would have been proud.

When it Absolutely, Positively, has to be Destroyed Overnight: This descriptive U.S. Marine saying means that the Corps is the answer when overnight destruction is the goal. U.S. Marines adapted this saying from a commercial delivery service slogan which "absolutely, positively" guaranteed delivery overnight.

When you want it done right, you send the Marines! This is another U.S. Marine Corps saying that was *borrowed* from a commercial source. In this case, a greeting card company had a slogan that encouraged customers to "send the very best." An instant match! The U.S. Marines garnered another credo.

Peace, through Superior Firepower: Marines, by profession, are warriors. Their combat skills are honed. Their combat tools are lethal. How else would they maintain world peace?
    True, some Marines prefer to fight with their Ka-Bars and E-tools, just to conserve ammo. But if you need sheer firepower, day or night, call the right number: 1-800-MARINES.

What part of *Marine* don't you understand? The bittersweet refrain from a ballad of lost love gave rise to this Marine Corps saying. Marine professionalism speaks for itself. ***Ooo-rah!***

Hey-diddle-diddle, right up the middle: *Marine-speak* for an attack in which Marine Warriors (1) conduct a frontal assault, (2) kill the enemy and his cohorts and let The Deity sort them out, and (3) then go home and let the Army do the occupying.

Heroes get remembered, but Legends live forever: Most heroes have their proverbial 15 minutes of fame. On the other hand, Legends never die. Remember the mythical GySgt. Hartman shouting to his Marines in *Full Metal Jacket*: ". . . and that means *YOU* will live forever!" (See the chapter, "Fighting Words from U.S. Marines," for more detail.)

When in doubt, empty the magazine! Better safe than sorry. If in doubt, just do it! Excellent combat advice. Remember, warriors *never* carry too much ammo on patrol or ambush.

{Nobody ever drowned in sweat:
{The more you sweat in training, the less you bleed in combat:
{Scars are the tattoos of the brave:
{Losers quit when they feel pain.   Marines quit when the
    mission is accomplished:
{Pain is just weakness leaving the body:
{Pain is temporary. Marine Pride is forever:
These six U.S. Marine slogans cut to the heart of the Marine ethos. By profession, Marines are warriors. Fighting is their purpose in life, their calling. When not in combat, Marines train for combat. Their Warrior Culture is their way of life.

In combat training (*if* you could call it that) the U.S. Navy *stops* when pain *starts*. The U.S. Army gives rigorous combat training a try, but backs off when its sensitivity counselors think someone might break a nail or get dirty. The U.S. Air Force does an adequate job in training as long as it is not (1) too hot, or (2) too cold, or (3) too tiring, or (4) on a weekend, or (5) in the rain, or (6) in the dark.

True warriors, U.S. Marines, "train through the pain" under all circumstances in preparation for combat. Marines use the slogans, above, as verbal badges of honor. These slogans are more than mere words. They are combat-proven principles for survival and victory in battle. *Ooo-rah!*

One good deal after another: No one seems to know the origin of this Marine Corps saying. Yet, it was in use during the wars in Korea, Vietnam, and the "land of sand."

You have to have *been there* to understand. A Marine Warrior who survives a perilous combat mission, and then gets *another* equally perilous combat mission, often remarks with a shrug, "One good deal after another." This is the warrior's way of announcing to the world that he can hack it, he packs the gear, no problem, his Corps offers "one good deal after another."

A letter of reprimand is better than no mail at all: The war in Vietnam featured a host of overzealous Marine Corps helicopter crews. One dark night in 1967, in a sky illuminated by enemy tracers, one Marine pilot in HMM-361 went far, far "beyond the call." Although his helicopter got shot to splinters, he and his crew somehow survived.

The next morning the aerial adventurer faced his superior's wrath. After a nifty "rug dance" he retired to his tent. That night, under cover of darkness, the side of the tent got spray-painted with a flippant philosophy: "A letter of reprimand is better than no mail at all." (This now-famous statement has been attributed to either Roger "Duke" Herman, Ron "Goody the Louse" Goodwin, or Norm "Whizzer" Whitbeck; none of whom will 'fess up.)

This devil-may-care attitude captured the imagination of Marines worldwide. To this day, when a Marine gets chastised for some actual or perceived blunder, the response is standard. After the "rug dance" the tongue-in-cheek explanation is the same: "A letter of reprimand is better than no mail at all."

Old Corps, New Corps, Hard Corps: In the Marine Corps, old-timers speak fondly to young Marines about the "Old Corps." The young Marines are quick to respond, "Old Corps, New Corps, Hard Corps." In other words, time does not change their Corps. All Marines are elite warriors, all *Hard Corps*.

You can tell a Marine -- but you can't tell him much: Although proud and patriotic, Marines are as stubborn as mules. Hard-headed! Pig-headed! Jar-headed! When you are the best, it is hard to be humble, hard to take advice.

<u>USMC -- America's 911</u>: Since 1775, a simple statement of fact needing no further explanation.

<u>Esprit de Corps</u>: In the U.S. Marine Corps, this is the fighting *spirit* of the Brotherhood of Marines. It is rooted in pride, honor, loyalty, and an unparalleled tradition of success in battle.

<u>Selected Marine Corps Recruiting Slogans</u>: The Marine Corps needs roughly 40,000 new recruits each year. To pick the right recruits, the *potential* Marines, the Corps selects from only the cream of America's young men and women.

Even a casual observer sees that Marine recruiting tactics differ from those used by other American military services. The Marine Corps recruiting posters, television advertisements, and slogans do not tout college tuition assistance (although such funds *are* available). They do not advertise travel to exotic lands. The Corps does not emphasize training that, later in life, will supposedly pave the way to success in the civilian business world.

Instead, the Marine Corps recruiting advertisements tout the *challenge* of their Warrior Culture. Maybe, just maybe, the potential recruit can measure up. Maybe the high school or college football star can become a *real* warrior, a warrior in both mind and body. Many try, and many evolve into U.S. Marines.

Yet, many other good men fail to make the cut, for example, the heavyweight boxing champion of the world. Without question, Riddick Bowe was a warrior: six feet, five inches tall; 235 pounds. The professional boxer seemed to have it all. He had won his first 31 fights, knocking out all but two of his opponents. Next, in November 1992 he had whipped Evander Holyfield to win the undisputed heavyweight championship of the world. Bowe earned millions in the ring, and then he retired. Yet, one childhood dream eluded him: the title of United States Marine.

Still in his prime at age 29, Bowe enlisted in the Corps. On 10 February 1997 he went to boot camp at Parris Island: Platoon 1036, Charlie Company, 1st Battalion. But after just 11 days, the dream ended on 21 February. Bowe was a tough man, a *good* man. But he did not make the cut in the Corps. In less than two weeks the Marine Corps training program had knocked out the former heavyweight champion of the world. Three years later in April 2000, Bowe wistfully reminisced to a news reporter for *The Detroit News*: "I'd give a million dollars to be a Marine."

Marine Corps training is tough, both mentally and physically. One must be *reborn* in body, mind, and spirit to *earn the title*. The Corps asks each prospective recruit the same question: "What makes you think you can become a United States Marine?" Maybe, just maybe, the prospective recruit has the mental discipline and physical endurance to evolve into a Marine Warrior.

Some of the recent Marine Corps recruiting slogans are listed below. There are no promises, only the *challenge*:

U.S. Marines. No short cuts, no promises, no compromises.

Nobody likes to fight, but somebody has to know how. The Marines are looking for a few good men.

Go Boldly where A Few Good Men have gone before.

The Marine Corps Builds Men - Body - Mind - Spirit.

We don't promise you a rose garden. The Marines are looking for a few good men.

We are the Marines! The Few! The Proud!

U.S. Marines. The change is forever.

If everybody could get in the Marines, it wouldn't be the Marines.

We're Looking for a Few Good Men.

The Marines are looking for a few good men.

U.S. Marines. We fight for each other, honor, and our Corps.

If you want to fight, join the Marines.

First in the fight. Always Faithful. Be a U.S. Marine!

Send in the Marines!

Time Tested. U.S. Marines.

The United States Marine Corps Builds Men.

The Marine Corps builds men. Ask a Marine.

Ask a Marine Officer.

The lifeblood of our Corps is the individual Marine.

After years of fitting in, maybe it's time to stand out. Marines!

Superior thinking has always overwhelmed superior force.
Marine Officer! The Few, The Proud, The Marines.

Since 1775: Making Marines, Winning Battles.

The change is forever. Marines. The Few. The Proud.

The Marine Corps makes no promises. It simply offers recruits
and officer candidates the challenge to "be one of us." The title,
United States Marine, cannot be bought or inherited. It cannot be
bestowed upon one who *joins* the Marine Corps. Only after
earning the title can one enter the storied Brotherhood of Marines.

Marine Corps League: MGen. John A. Lejeune, the fighting
thirteenth Commandant of the Marine Corps, founded the Marine
Corps League in 1923. Congress later chartered this exclusive
League on 4 August 1937. The Marine Corps League offers
membership to all honorably discharged, active duty, and reserve
Leathernecks of all ranks. The Mission Statement reads:

Members of the Marine Corps League join together in
camaraderie and fellowship for the purpose of preserving the

traditions and promoting the interests of the United States Marine Corps. This is accomplished by banding together those who are now serving in the United States Marine Corps and those who have been honorably discharged from that service; voluntarily aiding and rendering assistance to all Marines and former Marines and to their widows and orphans, and by perpetuating the history of the United States Marine Corps through fitting acts to observe the anniversaries of historical occasions of particular interest to Marines.

First and foremost, the League promotes the interests of the Corps. All else is secondary. With over 850 active detachments in the United States and overseas, a Marine Warrior usually can find a detachment close at hand.

One does not have to be a dues-paying member to enjoy League hospitality at local detachments. Camaraderie takes many forms, often including generous assortments of various libations. Under such circumstances the war stories fly thick and fast. Usually "the first liar doesn't stand a chance."

A National Commandant heads the League, and 14 elected national staff officers serve as trustees. Day to day, an Executive Director runs the national headquarters staff from offices in Fairfax, Virginia. The League is classified as a veterans/military service organization. Contributions are tax deductible.

General Orders for Sentries: The eleven General Orders for sentries never change. They constitute the unyielding bedrock upon which Marines enforce military security in the United States and throughout the world. General Orders dictate the conduct of all Marines on guard duty. These orders apply to all Marines at all bases and outposts in time of peace, and in time of war.

Marine recruits in boot camp must memorize these General Orders. Woe be unto the unfortunate recruit who can not shout out, verbatim and without hesitation, all eleven of them. Such a recruit will incur a firestorm of wrath from his Drill Instructor. There is sound logic for this rigid training. The eleven General

Orders will guide each Marine throughout his years in the Corps:

1. To take charge of this post and all government property in view.

2. To walk my post in a military manner, keeping always on the alert and observing everything that takes place within sight or hearing.

3. To report all violations of orders I am instructed to enforce.

4. To repeat all calls from posts more distant from the guardhouse than my own.

5. To quit my post only when properly relieved.

6. To receive, obey, and pass on to the sentry who relieves me, all orders from the commanding officer, officer of the day, and officers and noncommissioned officers of the guard only.

7. To talk to no one except in line of duty.

8. To give the alarm in case of fire or disorder.

9. To call the corporal of the guard in any case not covered by instructions.

10. To salute all officers and all colors and standards not cased.

11. To be especially watchful at night and, during the time for challenging, to challenge all persons on or near my post and to allow no one to pass without proper authority.

Code of Conduct: During the Korean War in the early 1950s, the Chinese Army and North Korean Army captured some American military men. These American prisoners then faced a deadly new enemy, the *Eastern World's* POW environment.

For the American prisoners, brutal torture, random genocide, lack of food, absence of medical aid, and subhuman treatment became the daily norm. Many of the Americans found that their training had not prepared them for this *new battlefield*.

After the war the American armed forces jointly developed a Code of Conduct. The President of the United States approved this written code in 1955. The six articles of the code constitute a comprehensive guide for all American military forces in time of war, and in time of peace. The articles of the code embrace (1) general statements of dedication to the United States and to the cause of freedom, (2) conduct on the battlefield, and (3) conduct as a prisoner of war.

The Code of Conduct is not a part of the Uniform Code of Military Justice (UCMJ). Instead, the Code of Conduct constitutes a personal action mandate for members of the American armed forces throughout the world:

Article I: I am an American, fighting in the armed forces which guard my country and our way of life. I am prepared to give my life in their defense.

Article II: I will never surrender of my own free will. If in command I will never surrender the members of my command while they still have the means to resist.

Article III: If I am captured, I will continue to resist by all means available. I will make every effort to escape and aid others to escape. I will accept neither parole nor special favors from the enemy.

Article IV: If I become a prisoner of war, I will keep faith with my fellow prisoners. I will give no information nor take part in any action which might be harmful to my comrades. If I am senior, I will take command. If not, I will obey the lawful orders of those appointed over me and will back them up in every way.

Article V: When questioned, should I become a prisoner of war, I am required to give name, rank, service number, and date of birth. I will evade answering further questions to the utmost of my ability. I will make no oral or written statements disloyal to my country and its allies or harmful to their cause.

Article VI: I will never forget that I am an American, responsible for my actions, and dedicated to the principles which made my country free. I will trust in my God and in the United States of America.

Memorial Day: The first *Decoration Day* was 30 May 1868, three years after the end of the American Civil War.

Gen. John A. Logan, USA, commander of the Grand Army of the Republic, began this annual day of remembrance. He ordered soldiers at *Army* posts to decorate the graves of fallen Civil War comrades with flowers and a "suitable ceremony." The order also required that flags be flown at half mast until noon.

Decoration Day later got a new name, Memorial Day. On this day the nation now honors those killed-in-action from all branches of the armed forces. This day of honor has been further expanded to include all wars and conflicts in which American servicemen have made the Supreme Sacrifice for their country.

Since the late 1950s on the Thursday before Memorial Day, the U.S. Army has placed small American flags at each of the quarter-million-plus graves in Arlington National Cemetery. The Army also stands guard in the cemetery through Memorial Day to ensure that the flags remain in place.

In 1968 (the height of the hippie and flower-power generation), Congress changed the observance date from 30 May to the last Monday in May. However, in 1999, bills were introduced in both the House of Representatives and the Senate, proposing restoration of 30 May as the day of observance.

According to tradition, Memorial Day is observed by placing flowers or small flags on the graves of American servicemen who have fallen in battle. Americans are encouraged to visit military memorials and to fly flags at half mast until noon. They also are asked to fly the relatively new "POW/MIA" flag per the 1998 Defense Authorization Act. Further, all Americans are asked to participate in a "Moment of Remembrance" at 3:00 pm and pledge to aid the families of the honored dead.

In many of the southern states, in addition to the national Memorial Day, citizens also observe Confederate Memorial Day. On this day they honor the Confederate soldiers, sailors, and Marines who died in battle during the American Civil War, 1861-1865. Because Confederate Memorial Day is an individual *state* holiday, each state may select its day of observance. Confederate Memorial Day is observed in Florida, Georgia, Missouri, and Mississippi on 26 April; in South Carolina and North Carolina on 10 May; and in Alabama on the last Monday in April. It is observed in Virginia on 30 May; in Kentucky, Tennessee, and Louisiana on 3 June (the birthday of Jefferson Davis, CSA President); and in Texas on 19 January (the birthday of Gen. Robert E. Lee, CSA).

Veterans Day: After four years of carnage in Europe the giant cannons finally fell silent. At 11:00 am on 11 November (the 11th hour, of the 11th day, of the 11th month) 1918, the Allies and Germany signed an armistice. The Great War, The World War, The War to End War, mercifully came to an end.

The whole world rejoiced. Thereafter the eleventh day of November became *Armistice Day* in most of the western world. In Canada it became known as *Remembrance Day*. In the United States, Congress officially recognized Armistice Day in 1926. Twelve years later, 11 November was declared a national holiday.

Three decades and two wars later, America realized that world order had been equally preserved by veterans of World War II and the Korean War. Consequently, Dwight D. Eisenhower, the U.S. President, signed legislation that changed the name of Armistice Day to Veterans Day in 1954.

In 1968 (the flower-power generation was hard at work again), Congress changed the day of observance to the fourth Monday in October. Veterans Day had temporarily become just another long three-day weekend. Therefore, the reason for the holiday was soon forgotten by many civilians.

Fortunately the public outcry rose steadily over the next ten years. Finally bowing to public pressure, Congress reversed itself in 1978. The eleventh day of November again became the day on which Americans observe Veterans Day.

By law, Veterans Day is set aside to honor our nation's military veterans, both living and dead, who served in time of war. The focal point for national observance is the Tomb of the Unknown Soldier (often called the "Tomb of the Unknowns") in Arlington National Cemetery. At 11:00 am on 11 November, a color guard that includes all four military services executes "Present Arms." The President of the United States lays a wreath upon the tomb, steps back, and salutes. A bugler plays *Taps*. A grateful nation has not forgotten.

Tomb of the Unknown Soldier (Tomb of the Unknowns): After World War I, Rev. David Railton visited a military cemetery in France. There, he knelt beside the graves of hundreds of British soldiers who had been killed in battle during The War to End War. Rev. Railton noted a grave marked only by a wooden cross. Upon the small cross was handwritten: "An unknown British soldier of the Black Watch."

Rev. Railton proposed that the unidentified soldier be brought home to England. The British government agreed, and the project took on a life of its own. Amid much ceremony, the soldier was disinterred in France. With full military honors, he was returned to England and laid to rest in Westminster Abbey on 11 November 1920. The state memorial service included an honor guard of British soldiers who had been awarded the Victoria Cross, England's highest award for valor. The tomb inscription reads:

A British Soldier Who Fell In The Great War 1914-1918
For King And Country

Another such gesture of honor took place in France. An unidentified French soldier who had been killed in The Great War was reinterred at the Arc de Triomphe.

The commanding general of American forces in France learned of these projects while they were still in the planning stages. He proposed a similar American plan to the U.S. Army Chief of Staff. The United States approved the reinterrment of an "American unknown soldier" during the 66th Congress on 4 March 1921.

The remains of an unidentified American combatant (there were

hundreds from which to choose) were disinterred in France. On 11
November 1921, then *Armistice Day*, the mortal remains of this
American Patriot entered their final resting place, a marble tomb on
the Plaza of the Memorial Amphitheater in Arlington National
Cemetery. The tomb is inscribed with these words:

Here Rests In Honored Glory An American Soldier
Known But To God

On Memorial Day in 1958 two more unidentified American war
dead were interred at the tomb. One had been killed in World War
II, and the other had sacrificed his life for his country during the
war in Korea.

Twenty-six years later in 1984 an unidentified American killed
during the war in Vietnam was interred beside the others. He
would remain there only 14 years. Because of DNA analysis and
other new identification techniques, this American was eventually
identified as Lt. Michael Blassie, USAF. In 1998 his family chose
to remove his remains and bury them elsewhere.

Today the Tomb of the Unknown Soldier is often called the
Tomb of the Unknowns. Here the interred unidentified American
combatants now represent all of the missing and unidentified men
who have fallen in battle in the service of their country. Many
families whose son, father, uncle, husband, or brother never
returned home from conflict abroad make frequent visits to the
Tomb of the Unknown Soldier.

Since 1937 the tomb has been guarded 24 hours per day by "The
Old Guard," the ceremonial 3rd Army Infantry. Inclusion in this
elite unit is one of the highest honors the U.S. Army can bestow
upon a soldier. The ritual "changing of the guard" each hour
during the day, and each two hours at night, is among the most
solemn military ceremonies in the United States.

Marine Warriors
and
"Air America"

Any gung-ho U.S. Marine knows, or surely has heard, something about "Air America." Maybe he has read the well-documented book. It was originally published in Great Britain in 1979 under the title, *The Invisible Air Force: The True Story of the CIA's Secret Airlines.* Avon Books republished this riveting saga in the United States in 1985 under a new title, **Air America**.

Many modern-day U.S. Marines have seen the childish "action-adventure" motion picture, *Air America.* Supposedly based on the book, the movie degenerated into a satirical farce aimed at legions of teenagers. It was devoid of any semblance of reality.

Other Marine Warriors likely have heard the whispers and the rumors. Maybe they have listened to the old-timers. Maybe they have heard the tales of getting "sheep-dipped," tales of somehow exchanging the Marine Corps uniform for civilian clothes in order to fight for freedom abroad. Where does the truth lie?

The facts: At one time Air America was the largest "airline" in the entire world. The most aircraft. Unlimited finances. And the United States' clandestine Central Intelligence Agency (CIA) called all of the shots -- *Black Ops!*

First, a little background is necessary. Prior to World War II, Japan invaded hapless China. Desperate to stop the Japanese, the American government sent Claire L. Chennault and his "American Volunteer Group" to China. These *civilian volunteers*, the famous "Flying Tigers," flew their P-40 fighters against the Japanese Air Force during the struggle for the Chinese mainland.

After World War II ended in 1945, the United States still aided Generalissimo Chiang Kai-Shek in his new battle against the Chinese Communists. Using the basic framework of the American

Volunteer Group, the American government formed Civil Air Transport (CAT) in 1947. CAT operated a fleet of airplanes to support the war machine of the Chinese Nationalists.

CAT moved its headquarters to fortress Taiwan in 1950 after Free China set up its government there. During the Korean War the American aircrews of CAT flew a host of clandestine missions that will never find their way into American history books. CAT also began flying regular passenger routes to Tokyo, Bangkok, Manila, and locations throughout the Far East.

The shadowy CAT was "obtained" by the American CIA after the Korean War. Flying under the names of (1) Civil Air Transport, (2) Southern Air Transport, (3) Air America, and (4) Air Asia Ltd., the government "airline" operated under the direction of the CIA in the western Pacific and in Asia throughout the 1950s.

When the French were on the ropes in Indochina and the American military could not officially intervene, CAT took over. Its aerial mercenaries repeatedly swooped down into the lethal firestorm at Dien Bien Phu. For public consumption the aircraft and mercenaries of CAT never existed. Yet, the secrets began to trickle out. In his world-acclaimed book, *Hell in a Very Small Place*, Dr. Bernard B. Fall explained:

> Twenty-four of the twenty-nine C-119s flying as part of the French supply operations had American crews under contract to the Taiwan-based Civil Air Transport.

When the war in Cambodia, Laos, and Vietnam heated up in the 1960s, the CIA consolidated its "airlines" under the single name of *Air America*. The CIA recruited some of its pilots and cargo-kickers from civilian sources, but most of the CIA's mercenary airmen came directly from the American military.

U.S. Marines flocked to join the mercenary band. Air America made it patently clear whom they wanted: "The most highly skilled, adventurous, and patriotic aviation personnel who could be found."

Aggressive Marine Corps pilots of that era had the "unofficial opportunity" to apply for reassignment to Air America. Those who were accepted got "sheep-dipped" and vanished. When next seen, they would be "civilians" flying meticulously maintained silver airplanes and helicopters in Asia. In small black letters on the fuselage of each aircraft were the words, "Air America."

The motto of Air America was simple: "Anything, Anytime, Anywhere." *Rice* was rice. *Hard rice* was ammo. *SAR* was an easy way to get yourself killed in Cambodia, Laos, China, North Vietnam, South Vietnam, or wherever. It did not matter. When you do not officially exist, there are no restrictions.

Most of the Marine Corps' sheep-dipped pilots and aircrewmen survived. One by one they mysteriously surfaced years later and somehow -- *presto!* -- automatically returned to active duty in the Corps. No questions, no comments.

For the United States the war in Indochina ended in 1975. Air America more or less disbanded. In *retirement* its mercenary patriots formed the Air America Club. Official recognition, which had never before existed, would come 12 years later.

Today the ***Air America Memorial*** stands at the McDermott Library at the University of Texas in Dallas. It was dedicated on 30 May 1987 by William E. Colby, the former Director of the CIA. He titled his dedication address, "Courage in Civilian Clothes." Beginning alphabetically with the name Robert P. Abrams, the bronze memorial lists each of the 242 *civilians* who lost their lives while flying with Air America. The inscription begins:

> This memorial is dedicated to the aircrews and ground support personnel of Civil Air Transport, Air America, Air Asia, and Southern Air Transport, who died while serving the cause of freedom in Asia from 1947 to 1975 . . . .

William P. Clements Jr., Governor of Texas, offered his greetings to the hundreds of Air America survivors who attended. He wrote: "It is high time that these brave individuals be honored."

Although Ronald Reagan, President of the United States, was not present, he sent a personal letter on White House stationery:

> . . . Unsung and unrecognized, each of you confronted danger and endured terrible hardships, and each of you rose to the challenge; you never faltered. Although free people everywhere owe you more than we can hope to repay, our greatest debt is to your companions who gave their last full measure of devotion. Just as their names are inscribed on this memorial, so

their memories are inscribed in our hearts . . . God bless you, and God bless America.

But has the CIA's airline (by whatever name) *really* faded away? The United States' intelligence community remains on the job. Somewhere in the world there is always a challenge for American adventurers, patriots, or "a few good men."

Insight is found in the "Introduction" to *The Invisible Air Force: The True Story of the CIA's Secret Airlines.* The author of the book, Christopher Robbins, makes it patently clear:

> Air America is a company incorporated in Delaware, but it is also a generic name used to describe all of the CIA air activities . . . There is a web of dozens of CIA airlines throughout the world which should perhaps go under the title, CIA AIR. But, that is a logo you will not find anywhere.

In the mid-1980s in Nicaragua, Contra rebels battled the ruling Sandinistas. On 5 October 1986 the Sandinistas managed to shoot down a shadowy arms-carrying supply plane. Aircraft documents found at the crash site revealed that the plane was owned by Southern Air Transport (sound familiar?). The pilot, William Cooper, and the copilot, Wallace "Buzz" Sawyer, were killed. The only surviving crewmember turned out to be a U.S. Marine Corps veteran, Eugene Hausenfauss. Another U.S. Marine, gung-ho Col. Oliver North, eventually took the then-public "Contra" flak, and in so doing he evolved into a true American hero.

So, does Air America still live today? (No problem, just review public listings of charter air carriers.) In times of international crisis, and in the ongoing battle against terrorism and tyranny, can America still count on *A Few Good Men* out of uniform? (Hint: this is a no-brainer.)

A Few Good Extremists
(Thank you, Sara Lister)

A Few Good Men. Those four prophetic words first described the Brotherhood of Marines over 200 years ago. In Boston on 20 March 1779, Capt. William Jones, Continental Marines, had advertised for "*a few good men*" to enlist in the Corps for duty aboard Continental Navy warships.

Recently in 1997 a new moniker reared its head: "*A Few Good Extremists*." Was this praise, or insult? Was it on target, or totally off base? Marine Warriors, take a look at the facts:

The culprit (or *prophet*, depending upon your viewpoint) was Sara E. Lister. At the time she held a lofty post, Assistant Secretary of the Army for Manpower and Reserve Affairs. Lister favored *gender-norming* the U.S. Army.

Meanwhile, other political activists were already hard at work trying to feminize the Army. Under the silly COO (Consideration of Others) program, soldiers were forced to endure *coo*-sensitivity sessions. Like locusts, swarms of "politically correct" civilian facilitators swarmed onto Army bases. These deluded zealots began instilling their concepts of "common courtesy, decency, and sensitivity to the feelings of others" in soldiers of the *new Army*. Training for combat got diluted into near irrelevance.

The Army found a like-minded female professor at Duke University, based upon her Law Review article. It proposed that the Army abandon its "construct of masculinity" and, instead, focus on "compassion and understanding" (nothing about *fighting* for one's country). The professor became the Army's new "Special Assistant on Gender Relations."

Tragically, it got worse, much worse. When not actively ridiculing the warrior ethos, civilian COO advocates turned U.S. Army basic training into a virtual summer camp. Courtesy, not combat, became the overriding concern. Kinder, gentler Army drill sergeants could no longer shout and berate recruits. On the obstacle course, if climbing the wall looked too intimidating, a soldier could elect to walk around it. Many soldiers who began training in good athletic condition actually became de-conditioned by the lack of exertion. Training for fighting and combat would not be appropriate for *decent* soldiers. Instead, the *new Army* would revolve around a warm and fuzzy notion of "fairness."

At the time most Marine Warriors silently resented the plague being forced upon their brothers-in-arms in the Army. But that resentment changed to anger the day when Ms. Lister verbally attacked the U.S. Marine Corps.

On 26 October 1997, Lister attended a conference in Baltimore, Maryland. The Institute for Strategic Studies at Harvard University sponsored this elite think-tank. At the conference, well attended and documented by the media, Lister announced: "The Marines are extremists." Then she added: "Whenever you have extremists, you've got some risks of total disconnection with society." Lister continued by calling the Marines "dangerous." Then she scoffed at the Marines' "checkerboard fancy uniforms and stuff."

Big mistake! The flak came from all quarters, fast and furious. The Commandant of the Marine Corps, Gen. Charles C. Krulak, immediately fired back. He stated that Lister's remarks "summarily dismiss 222 years of sacrifice and dedication" and "dishonor the hundreds of thousands of Marines whose blood has been shed in the name of freedom." Conrad Burns, U.S. Senator and Marine veteran, wrote to Lister: "Your remarks were an affront to every Marine . . . you have impugned all who have served in the United States Armed Forces and died for the very freedoms you enjoy." Representative John Hostettler, outspoken as always, noted that Lister's "blatant disrespect for the U.S. Marines makes her unfit for the position she holds." Herman Voelkner, a retired Army officer, wrote about Ms. Lister: "She shows herself as lacking even a basic understanding of the military ethos."

The U.S. House of Representatives agreed. After angry speeches denouncing Ms. Lister, the House passed a resolution demanding her removal from office. Ms. Lister did not wait to be fired. After apologizing to Gen. Krulak, she resigned.

As radio newsman Paul Harvey would say, in a minute you'll hear "the rest of the story." True, Lister was gone. The sarcastic nature of her remarks had insulted Congress, the U.S. Marine Corps, and the American public. But could it be that Lister was actually on to something?

Despite her sarcastic manner, Lister was correct about one thing. Marine Warriors, when plying their professional warfighting trade, are "***dangerous extremists***." Through *extreme* combat prowess, Marines pose a clear ***danger*** to the enemies of our nation. Toby Hughes, an Air Force fighter pilot with combat experience, put it this way: "I never knew many Marines who were only a 'little' dangerous. Most of them seem to be a LOT dangerous. That, I think, is the right idea." *The Washington Post*, describing the Marines and their "white-hot determination honed by long years of training," would later put the Marine Corps into perspective:

> They are America's warriors, and they are ready . . . These are United States Marines, and they are *dangerous*. They are poised, if and when the order comes, to wreak systematic havoc on the enemies of their country.

Another writer described the U.S. Marines as "*extremely* fit, *extremely* faithful, *extremely* patriotic." In later years, MSgt. Vincent Yates, USMC, would explain it another way: "Every nation fears us, because they know we'll get the job done."

The storied battle history of the U.S. Marine Corps speaks for itself. With their extreme pride, heritage, and Warrior Culture, the Marines revere patriotism and sacrifice as a way of life. Marine Warriors believe in each other, their Corps, and their Country.

Marines look upon service to their nation as a God-given opportunity, not a burden. They believe "doing more with less" to be a virtue, not a vice. Marines cling to old-fashioned concepts like honor, integrity, duty, and military prowess. These may be *extremist* views to the pitiful apostles of "political correctness." Yet, for Marines there is no other way to serve their Country.

Now you know "the rest of the story." Although Ms. Lister's sarcasm was not acceptable, she was right on target in one regard. Marines are ***extremists***, and Marines are ***dangerous***. One noted author explained it this way: "In fact, it was this ***dangerous patriotic extremism*** that powered the Marines at Belleau Wood, Guadalcanal, Chosin Reservoir, and Hue City."

We live in a troubled world. It is only a matter of time before civilian American hostages are again taken, or an American embassy is surrounded by armed lunatics, or some despot enslaves helpless civilians. It is not a question of *if*. It is a question of *when*. And when it does happen, the hostages will not pray for the arrival of kinder, gentler rescuers. They will not offer prayers for rescue by *coo*-ing advocates of courtesy and decency. They will not pray for rescuers guided by principles of politeness, understanding, and compassion, nor will they pray for the arrival of rescuers who opted to walk around the wall in training.

Certainly, the hostages *will* pray. But they will pray for rescue by elite professional warriors. They will pray for the arrival of **dangerous military extremists**. They will pray for the lethal thunder of gung-ho and hard-charging United States Marines!

Fortunately for America, U.S. Marines are **extremists**! U.S. Marines are **dangerous**! They always have been, they always will be. And as long as America needs defending, America will need *A Few Good Extremists*. The Few. The Proud. The Marines.

Only The Deity can forgive the enemies of our great nation. The U.S. Marines can not. The Marines just arrange the meeting.

The Marine Warrior's Rules for Life

For each United States Marine, life and service constitute a trust, a responsibility, and an opportunity. But before we set out to change the world, we should start at home.

The person we see in the mirror each morning is the person with whom we should begin. The most crucial person with whom we must live is ourselves. In that regard, we must make sure that we remain in good company. If we heed these basic *rules for life*, we will have taken a giant step in that direction:

Dare to be different. If all think alike, none are really thinking.

In matters of *conscience*, ignore the majority.

Shun unanimity when it equates to ethical or moral cowardice.

Right or wrong, your silence equals your consent.

Avoid any philosophy supported by an absence of courage.

The pathway to failure lies in trying to please everyone.

Your *character* is what you are, alone in the dark. Your character is your *destiny*.

If you always tell the truth, you never have to remember anything.

Believe in, and sacrifice for, *a cause greater than self.*

Remember that (1) small minds discuss people, (2) average minds discuss events, but (3) great minds discuss ideas.

Never wrestle with a pig; never argue with an idiot.

Tilting at windmills hurts you more than it hurts the windmills.

Remember, no monument was ever erected to honor a cynic.

In interpersonal matters, apply The Golden Rule.

It is *great* to be great. It is *greater* to be human.

Never sneer at anyone's dreams, for dreams may be all they have.

The better part of your life consists of your friendships.

Never allow a little dispute to injure a great friendship.

Count your wealth by your friends, not your dollars.

Great love, like any great achievement, involves great risk.

Dare to dare, for nothing worthwhile is achieved without risk.

Judge an achievement by what you had to risk to get it.

The greater the potential reward, the greater the guaranteed risk.

Often, not getting what you want can be a fantastic stroke of luck.

The three keys to success: (1) vision (2) initiative (3) commitment.

Yesterday is history. Tomorrow is never guaranteed. Today is all you have to work with.

Never give up, never back down, never give in. Keep scratching.

-- Life is always in session. Are you always present? --

PART TWO

Happy Hour!

If you are allergic to lead, you would be wise to avoid combat.

Happy Hour Laws of Combat for Marine Infantry

The basic laws of combat never change! Marine Warriors must learn from the fatal mistakes of others. Otherwise, in combat they will not survive long enough to learn how to survive permanently.

Although basic laws of combat do not change, weapons do. In the beginning, combatants used their fists and teeth. Later they graduated to clubs and big rocks. Soon a sharpened club evolved into a spear. Then a sharpened rock, strapped to a stick, became a sophisticated war ax. Hi-tech stuff!

Swords and shields quickly followed. The long-bow and its arrows came next, and later the mechanized crossbow became an even more lethal and accurate killing machine. Then the Chinese stumbled across gunpowder, and the rest is history.

The modern-day Marine Grunt charges into battle while armed with a dizzying array of guns, mines, rockets, missiles, and electronic smart weapons. He races overland inside of lethal armored chariots. At his beck and call are flying machines of incredible speed and complexity that are ready to rain death and destruction down upon the bad guys and their evil cohorts.

Today, U.S. Marines are universally recognized as the premier warriors on the planet. Marines come in many sizes: skinny and mean, stout and mean, tall and mean, etc. Nonetheless, each has *earned the title* and lives within the eternal Brotherhood of Marines. Each of these modern-day American Samurai is a fierce warrior, a patriot, a lethal population control specialist who loves his Corps and Country.

Marines have evolved into revered American icons, the military elite of the world. They stormed Chapultepec Castle and seized *the halls of Montezuma*. They battered down the gates of the fortress at Derna on *the shores of Tripoli*. Marines fight!

These professional military extremists have the toughest mascot, the toughest boot camps and OCS, the best motivational shout, and the only military anthem that is a *hymn*.   They have the best fighting knife, the most *gungy* fighting slogans, the best leaders and warriors -- Chesty, Smedley, Manila John and company -- and the best toll-free phone number, 1-800-MARINES.

Each Marine has been trained as a Grunt, a rifleman, and each knows the lethal truth: "The deadliest weapon in the world is a Marine and his rifle." Marines also know that their revered Marine Corps War Memorial, rising from *hallowed ground* in Arlington, Virginia, is the most famous war memorial on Earth.

O.K., you Magnificent Grunts, Gyrenes, Jarheads, Devil Dogs, Leathernecks, or whatever! Listen up! Handed down through the ages, here are your laws of combat, your keys to staying alive and winning in battle.   These laws of combat apply to all Marine Warriors. However, they are genuine **combat commandments** for the legendary Marine Infantry. For your convenience these laws are grouped into six simple categories:

1. Combat Philosophy for Marine Infantry
2. The Dirty-Dozen "Rules of Firefights" for Marine Infantry
3. Combat Tactics for Marine Infantry
4. Combat Precautions for Marine Infantry
5. Combat Ironies for Marine Infantry
6. Barracks Wisdom for Marine Infantry

-- Combat Philosophy for Marine Infantry --

If you are allergic to lead, you would be wise to avoid combat.

In combat, any Marine Warrior who does not openly consider himself the best in the game is in the *wrong* game.

War does not decide who is right. War decides who is left.

There is only one overriding rule in warfare -- the winner always gets to make up the rules.

A Marine Warrior knows that *diplomacy* is the refined social art of saying "nice doggie" until he can find a bigger rock.

You may be able to win without fighting, and it is preferable. But it also is *harder*, and the enemy may not cooperate.

Sooner or later in life, every Marine Warrior has to die. The trick is to die young -- as late as possible.

Warriors live a rough life. Only the young die good.

The only warriors fit to live are those who are not afraid to die.

For civilians, to *err* is human, to *forgive* is divine. For Marine Warriors in combat, neither is acceptable.

Medals are OK. Having all your warrior brothers alive is better.

In combat, no matter how bad it gets, having all of your body parts intact and functioning makes it a good day.

When you win, nothing hurts!

When you win, you are entitled to the spoils of war. If you lose, you will not care.

Do not believe what they told you in grammar school. In the real world and in combat, violence solves *everything*.

To triumph in war, like in love, you must initiate contact.

It is much easier to forgive an enemy *after* you have killed him.

Only imbeciles and fools fight fair (and will not do so for long).

Fools trust their enemies. Skepticism is the mother of survival.

The "Law of the Bayonet" says that the guy with the bullets wins.

Forget that "the harder they fall" foolishness. The bigger the bad guys are, the harder they punch, choke, and kick.

When a warrior buddies-up for combat, he should avoid pacifists and cowards (those who think with their legs).

Marine Warriors should never trust the sniveling media whores. You have to "read between the lies."

Real warriors never get bogged down in a political war, where adversaries only shoot from the lip.

Hot garrison chow flown to the field is best. Hot field rations are better than cold field rations. Cold field rations are better than no food at all. Nonetheless, no food at all is still better than a cold rice ball a day, even though it may have little pieces of fish-head in it. ***Never surrender!***

A warrior's pack, however heavy, is lighter than a POW's chains.

{Know warfare, know peace and safety;
{No knowledge of warfare, no peace and safety.

Even the Boy Scouts have figured it out: "Be Prepared."

Between firefights, *care packages* from home are great.   Share everything, even the pound cake and cookies.

Without resupply, neither colonels nor corporals are combat ready.

For Marine Warriors in combat, air superiority is never a luxury.

Nonetheless, no one has yet discovered any type of *flying* that can prevent a Grunt from *walking*.

If you are convinced that you will lose, you are probably right.

In combat, last guys *do not* finish nice.

Day or night, incoming fire always has right-of-way.

Warriors who beat their swords into plowshares will end up plowing for those who do not.

Artillery lends dignity to what otherwise would be a vulgar brawl.

Marine Warriors in combat in the tropics never wear underwear. Only they can appreciate why.

C-4 can make a dull day fun.

The raw intensity of a War Story is *inversely* proportional to the combat experience of the storyteller (a good way to identify wannabes and other non-combatants).

The number of mosquitoes at any given location is *inversely* proportional to your remaining amount of repellant.

The probability of diarrhea is *directly* proportional to the square of the thistle content of the local vegetation.

The urgency of the need to urinate is (1) *inversely* proportional to the temperature and (2) *directly* proportional to the layers of clothing you have to remove.

The combat effectiveness of any unit is *inversely* proportional to the amount of starch in its cammies.

The weight of your pack is *directly* proportional to the cube of the time you have been humping it.

The severity of the inclement weather is *directly* proportional to the amount of time you must be out in it.

When geared-up, the intensity of your itch is *inversely* proportional to the length of your reach.

The complexity of electronics equipment is *inversely* proportional to the IQ of the civilian instructors.

In a firefight, the seriousness of your wound is *directly* proportional to the distance to the nearest deep hole.

In a firefight, the difficulty of hearing a shouted order is *directly* proportional to the consequences for failing to carry it out.

In a firefight, the intensity of enemy fire is *directly* proportional to the curiousness of the enemy's target.

When you have run out of everything except the bad guys, you definitely are in combat.

If they are shooting at you, it is a "high intensity conflict."

Always make sure somebody has a P-38 (for you new guys, a P-38 is a can opener -- and *more!*).

In war, winning is not always all it is cracked up to be -- the only genuine winner in the War of 1812 was Tchaikovsky (who would not be born for another 28 years).

In time of war, Hell hath no fury like a pacifist.

In combat, bad news may arrive in human waves.

Between firefights, letters from home are not always great. Both living and dying can hurt a lot.

If the sheltered REMFs are happy, the Marine Warriors in combat likely do not have what they need.

When it comes to War Stories, the farther the REMF storyteller was from the battle, the thicker the flak will be in his story.

In combat, discretion is the *bitter* part of valor.

Unfortunately, combat is not an efficient teacher. It gives the final test before presenting the lesson.

In combat a hero is no more brave than anyone else, but he is brave five minutes longer.

When you take a calculated risk in a life-and-death firefight, there usually are very few calculations.

Those who "live by the sword" will *die* when they attack gung-ho Marine Warriors who fight with automatic weapons.

In combat the only perfect science is called hindsight.

"Subject Matter Experts" and "Professionals" have their place, but never get married to their ideas. Remember that (1) professionals built the *Titanic*, while (2) rank amateurs built the ark.

He who dies with the most toys is, nonetheless, dead.

After the battle, reputation is valuable, but honor is priceless.

Remember, if all of our Marine Warrior brothers do not come home, none of us can ever fully come home.

-- The Dirty-Dozen "Rules of Firefights" for Marine Infantry --

1. Never be the idiot who shows up armed only with a knife.

2. Bring an automatic weapon. Better yet, bring two.

3. Bring all of your Marine Warrior brothers you can find, with all of *their* automatic weapons.

4. Bring *lots and lots* of ammo! It is cheap life insurance.

5. Have a good plan. Have a good back-up plan.

6. Make sure your weapons will fire *every time* (if angel-pee causes your weapons to jam, you will be terminally SOL).

7. If one of your weapons is a handgun, make sure its caliber begins with the numeral "4" or greater.

8. Any bad guy worth shooting is worth shooting several times.

9. Smoke and loud noise do not kill. Only hits count.

10. Remember that the "hey-diddle-diddle" tactic works only in the movies. Be sneaky, always cheat, always win.

11. The faster you kill the bad guys, the less shot you will get.

12. Taking prisoners is (1) time consuming, (2) troublesome, and is (3) not recommended. Always kill *all* of the bad guys (if they are dead, they will make poor witnesses).

-- Combat Tactics for Marine Infantry --

Do unto the enemy, and do it *first*.

If you do not strike first, you will be the first struck.

Speak softly, but *forget* the big stick. Carry a belt-fed weapon.

In combat, true happiness is always a belt-fed weapon.

In combat, always kill as many bad guys as you can. The ones you miss today may not miss you tomorrow.

If you can avoid it, never get into a fight without at least five times as much ammo as the bad guys.

In combat, it is better for you to hump extra ammo than for your buddy to fill out your paperwork for Graves Registration.

Ammo is relatively cheap. Your life is not. In combat you can **never** hump too much ammo.

If you have extra ammo, even in a firefight, share quickly. You may be on the short end the next time around.

In a firefight, pace yourself. Otherwise, sooner or later you *will* run out of ammo -- usually at the worst possible time.

In general, the more ammo you have, the better. Nonetheless, it may spoil your day if, in a firefight, the type of ammo you have the most of is for the type of weapon you have the least of.

If you can avoid it, never get into a fair fight.

When given a choice, fight smarter, not harder.

Do what the enemy does not want you to do.

If at first your well-planned attack does not succeed, do not try again. Try something *different.*

If trying something different does not work, call in an airstrike.

In any firefight, nobody cares what you did yesterday, or what you may do tomorrow. The only thing that matters is what you are doing **right now**.

Cover your warrior brothers, so they will be around to cover you.

In combat, stay close. The farther you are from your Marine Warrior brothers, the less likely it is that they can help you when you need them the most.

When you have the enemy on the ground, kick him.

In combat, never look back unless you intend to go that way.

In a firefight, if you see two colonels conferring, you likely have fallen back a little too far.

If in command in a crisis, give all orders verbally. Never create a document that could wind up in a "Pearl Harbor" file.

If attacked by a fanatical, well armed, and numerically superior enemy force, it may be helpful to ponder: "How would the Lone Ranger handle this?"

On patrol and ambush, (1) never stand when you can sit, (2) never sit when you can lie down, (3) never stay awake when you can sleep, and (4) get in a good bowel movement whenever you can.

At night in combat, hang on to your gear. If you drop it during a fight, you can often find your canteen and E-tool right at your feet, but your ammo and grenades are probably lost forever.

Curious looking objects attract fire. Never lurk behind one.

When outnumbered in a firefight, shooting the bad guys is more important than radioing your plight to some REMF, miles away, who is incapable of assisting you.

In a firefight, he who hesitates is lost -- forever.

In a firefight, delay is the deadliest form of denial.

On the keyboard of combat, keep one finger on the escape key.

Always know when to "get out of Dodge."

In a firefight, (1) one problem is a problem, (2) two problems means it is time to get out of Dodge, but (3) three problems often means it is *too late* to get out of Dodge.

In combat, "what" is more important than "why" (when you see a snake, do not fret over why it is there, just shoot it).

A good plan today is always better than a great plan tomorrow.

In combat, if something does not matter, it does not matter. The trick is to *make sure* that it does not matter.

On patrol and ambush, smart Marine Warriors always keep their eyes peeled, for he who sees first lives longest.

If you lose contact with the enemy, remember to look behind you.

Anything you do in combat can get you killed. Doing nothing will generally get you killed more quickly.

In a firefight, do *something*, even if it is wrong.

No matter how bad it gets, it is not over until it is over.

If you lose, and if you are still alive, do not lose the reason.

-- Combat Precautions for Marine Infantry --

Beware! Combat is always easier to get into than out of.

Once you are in the fight, it is too late to ponder whether or not it was a good idea.

Remember, you are not Superman, and you are not bulletproof.

Combat is not like Hollywood. In combat, getting shot *hurts*.

If you are in it, there is no such thing as a little firefight.

In combat, the best medal is the longevity medal.

In combat, prayer may not help, but it certainly can not hurt.

"Courage under fire" means that you are the only person who knows that you are afraid.

In a firefight, a (1) tie or a (2) split decision is not a viable option.

When you have run out of options in a firefight, if you think the enemy may be low on ammo, try to look unimportant.

Never try to draw fire. It irritates those around you.

In hi-tech, bio-weapon, and smart-weapon combat, there is no safety in numbers -- or in anything else.

Avoid all loud noises. There are few silent killers in combat.

Remember, the enemy may surrender, but his mines will not.

There are good plans, but there are no perfect plans. Beware, for your confidence may merely be your suspicion, asleep.

In combat, if everything is as clear as a bell, and things are going precisely as planned, look out! You are ripe for a surprise.

In combat a thorough mission briefing is a good idea, but do not get married to it. No plan has *ever* survived enemy contact, intact.

A warrior who thinks *small* bad guys can not be lethal in combat has never been in bed with a small rattlesnake.

When you have a clear choice in a crisis, opt for safety. That way, you will survive to be brave later on.

In combat, macho talk aside, *surviving* is more important than winning. You can only die once. But you can have many chances to win *if* you survive long enough to get them.

If your situation is desperate, it is too late to be serious.

He who hesitates under fire usually will not get another chance to.

If you suddenly find yourself in front of your Marine Warrior brothers in combat, they likely know something you do not.

When you are curled up deep in your hole, with mortars and

artillery and bombs exploding all around, you can bet your bottom dollar that no atheists are lurking nearby.

In combat, rash decisions often bleed consequences.

Anyone can charge an enemy machinegun emplacement, across open terrain, alone, in broad daylight -- once.

When the pin has been pulled, Mr. Grenade is no longer our friend.

The bursting radius (killing range) of any grenade is *always* greater than your jumping range.

In combat it is inadvisable to buddy-up with someone whose grenade throwing range is less than the grenade killing range.

In a firefight, if you are keeping your head while all around you are losing theirs, perhaps you should reevaluate the situation.

A sucking chest wound is bad. But on the other hand, (1) all wounds are bad, and (2) all wounds suck.

Food for thought: your weapons were made by the lowest bidder.

A non-posthumous Purple Heart only proves you were (1) smart enough to think of a plan, (2) crazy enough to try it, and (3) lucky enough to survive.

Getting outnumbered and surrounded by the enemy is *always* a bad idea. (But on the bright side, it is a unique opportunity to get rid of the heavy ammo you have been humping.)

Before any firefight, it is bad luck to be superstitious.

Any bad guy with a rifle is a better shot than you with a pistol.

In a firefight, the greatest danger is the company of scared people.

But, a good scare is usually more effective than good advice.

If your attack is known in advance, it should not take place.

The concept of "survival of the fittest" is invalidated when some would-be hero insists on putting himself in a position where he will soon get himself killed.

After the fray, it is better to be a live lamb than a dead lion.

To appreciate the value of a single minute, ask any combat veteran what his friend was doing a minute before he got killed.

Helicopter resupply pilots will see you. Attack pilots on a close air support run will not. Dig your hole a little deeper.

-- Combat Ironies for Marine Infantry --

No matter what you do, the bullet with your name on it will get you. So, also, can *random bullets* addressed "to whom it may concern" and *shrapnel* addressed to "occupant."

For each military action, there is an equal and opposite criticism.

When you have plenty of ammo, you never miss. When you are low on ammo, you can not hit squat.

The ammo you need *now* will be on the *next* chopper.

If you wear body armor, the enemy usually will miss that part.

In combat the only thing more accurate than incoming enemy fire is incoming friendly fire.

Most firefights occur at the junction of several maps. If you do not use paper maps, firefights occur when your batteries die.

In any wooded area at night, the sharp dead limbs on trees always will be at either (1) eye level or (2) groin level.

If you can not remember, the Claymore is pointed toward you.

Standard five-second fuses are so named because they burn in five seconds (plus or minus about four).

No combat-ready unit has ever passed inspection.

No inspection-ready unit has ever passed combat.

It is impossible to make any weapons system foolproof, because fools are deceptively ingenious.

Professional enemy soldiers are predictable. Unfortunately, the world is full of dangerous amateurs.

Combat is not like Hollywood. In combat the cavalry does not always come to the rescue.

Combat, like love, is not called off on account of darkness.

If the enemy is within range, generally, so are you.

Radar fails (1) at night, or (2) in inclement weather, or (3) both.

Radios fail when you desperately need fire support.

If you make it hard for the enemy to get in, you can not get out.

The enemy always mines the *easy* way out.

The easy way usually will get you killed.

The enemy diversion you ignore usually is his main attack.

The enemy will attack when two conditions are met: (1) when he is ready, and (2) when you are not.

The enemy will attack *most ferociously* under two conditions: (1) on the darkest night, and (2) during a rainstorm.

The retreating enemy *squad* your platoon thinks it is pursuing is often an enemy *reconnaissance team*, luring you back to its entrenched *regiment* -- locked, loaded, and waiting.

Often, *military intelligence* is a contradiction in terms.

Fortify your front, and the enemy will attack your rear.

If your ambush is properly set, the enemy will never arrive.

If you are sufficiently dug in, the enemy will never attack.

The enemy has a penchant for turning your mines into equal opportunity weapons.

Superior firepower always prevails -- sometimes.

Combat experience is usually what we call our combat mistakes.

Marine Warriors who take more than their fair share of objectives will get more than their fair share to take.

In combat, no order is so simple that it can not be misunderstood.

In a firefight, teamwork is essential. It gives the enemy someone else to shoot at.

The enemy never watches until you make a mistake.

If it worked in practice, it will fail in combat.

Things that must work together can not be shipped together.

-- Interchangeable parts *aren't*.

-- Friendly fire *isn't*.

-- Insect repellents *don't*.

-- Perfect plans *aren't* (and neither is the backup plan).

-- Recoilless rifles *aren't* (ask the idiot who stood behind one).

-- Waterproof clothing *isn't* (but it *does* retain perspiration).

-- Flash suppressors *do* (but only in the daytime).

-- Suppressive fires *won't* (except when they are directed onto abandoned positions).

-- Things that must be shipped together *aren't*.

-- Things that must work together *won't*.

Experience in combat is something you never have enough of until *after* you desperately need it.

The thing you need the most will be at the bottom of your pack.

If you need *n* crucial items from Supply, there will be *n-1* in stock.

If your attack looks easy, it usually is hard. If your attack looks hard, it usually is impossible.

A slipping gear will allow your M-203 grenade launcher to fire when you least expect it. This may make you quite unpopular with what is left of your unit.

Unfortunately, tracers work both ways.

No matter which way you march, it is uphill and into the wind.

You will always be downwind when toxic gas is used.

In combat, as in life, success occurs when you are alone. Failure occurs when everyone is watching.

Any stone in a boot migrates to the point of maximum pressure.

The weight of your pack can never remain uniformly distributed on the shoulder straps.

When hot garrison chow is flown to the field, it will rain.

In military intelligence, generally (1) the information you have is not what you want, (2) the information you want is not what you need, (3) the information you need is not available, and (4) everything depends on something else.

In combat, the side with the simplest uniform usually wins.

The crucial round will be a dud.

Military working dogs are trained to attack anything, including you.

About 15 percent of an intelligence report will be accurate and relevant. The trick is to figure out *which* 15 percent.

-- Barracks Wisdom for Marine Infantry --

Unfortunately, no Marine Warrior fights all of the time. Between battles and wars, he and his Marine brothers will retire in-the-rear-with-the-gear to rest and recuperate. There they will carouse, drink, brawl, and try to corrupt members of the opposite sex.

Warriors, your days in a barracks environment are fraught with potential peril. Here the *new enemy* smiles and shakes hands before stabbing you in the back. The soulless media whores, the mercenary purveyors of sensationalism and negativism, will leap at any opportunity to steal your honor. Worse yet, the parasitic liberal *politically correct* zealots will stop at nothing in attempts to drag you into the gutter of society with them. Therefore, all warriors in a barracks environment should remember:

When they can choose between a (1) *politically correct* cry-baby and a (2) true warrior, the sniveling media whores will always interview the cry-baby.

Those who torture animals and wet the bed are either sex perverts or staff pogues. Both should be avoided.

No decision, made in your absence, will be in your best interests.

Friends come and go, but enemies accumulate.

"You have the right to remain silent" is excellent advice.

Between wars, never delay (1) the end of a meeting, or (2) the start of Happy Hour.

Between wars, (1) girlfriends are fair game, but (2) wives are not.

Between wars, never let (1) a fool kiss you, or (2) a kiss fool you.

The six time-tested verbal responses calculated to *avoid responsibility or blame*, listed in descending order of preference:
   (1) Who, me?
   (2) I wasn't there.
   (3) I didn't do it.
   (4) Nobody saw me do it.
   (5) You can't prove a thing.
   (6) That's my story, and I'm sticking to it.

Happy Hour Laws of Combat
for
Marine Aviation

Some gung-ho Marine Warriors fight *above* the battlefield. For these aerial warriors, the Commandant added "in the air" to *The Marines' Hymn* in 1942.

The history of Marine Aviation is an immense sea of errors in which a few obscure truths may here and there be found. And like other occult techniques, aviation has a private jargon contrived to obscure its methods from non-practitioners.

Marine Aviation is not simple! Trying to fly without feathers was *never* easy. First came the hot air balloonists. No problem. They never killed anyone except themselves, from time to time. But on 17 December 1903, Wilbur and Orville started the aerial foolishness that still has us in trouble today. Because of those two culprits, aviation has gotten ever higher and faster, ever more complex and more dangerous.

In Marine Aviation, warriors soon learn that the most deadly enemy is not the bad guys. The biggest threat comes from our own flying machines that *screw* (helicopters) or *suck and blow* (airplanes) their way through the sky. Unfortunately, U.S. Marines have to *ride* or *fly* in these flimsy contraptions. For pilots and aircrewmen, the trick is to stay alive long enough to get the experience to enable them to stay alive a little longer. You unfortunate Grunts just along for the ride, ***think*** about it. Maybe humping the hills on foot is not so bad after all.

One who studies the aeronautical laws of combat may discover a possibility, however remote, of survival. These timeless truths for warriors are grouped into four categories:

1. Philosophy for Marine Aviation
2. Admonitions for Marine Aviation

3. Ironies of Marine Aviation
4. Infamous Military Aviation Predictions

-- Philosophy for Marine Aviation --

Gravity never loses. The best you can hope for is a draw.

Although fuel is a limited resource, gravity is forever.

In the ongoing battle between (1) Marine Corps aircraft going hundreds of miles per hour, and (2) mountains going zero miles per hour, the mountains have yet to lose.

The three aviation constants: (1) airspeed is *life*, (2) altitude is *life insurance*, and (3) fuel is *more* life insurance.

The only time you have too much fuel is when you are on fire.

A combat aircrew lives in a world of perfection -- or not at all.

If all you can see out of the cockpit window is the ground, going round and round, and all you can hear is screaming in the cabin, something likely is amiss.

The mechanics of flying are simple. If you push the stick forward, the houses get bigger. If you pull the stick back, the houses get smaller. Of course, if you pull the stick back *too far*, the houses *very rapidly* get bigger again.

Assumption is the mother of most crashes.

Military flying consists of hours and hours of boredom, interrupted by brief moments of stark terror.

All take-offs are optional. But landing, *somewhere*, is mandatory.

A Marine Corps aircraft can land anywhere -- once.

In combat, having a wingman is essential. He gives the enemy someone else to shoot at.

When returning to Earth at high speed, the probability of survival is *inversely* proportional to the angle of arrival (large angle of arrival, small probability of survival, and vice versa).

While flying, you usually do not know what you do not know.

It is better to look bad than to die. But in Marine Aviation it is easy to do both -- simultaneously.

There are (1) old combat aircrews, and there are (2) bold combat aircrews. But there are very few *old and bold* combat aircrews.

There is no such thing as a *routine* combat mission.

Superior pilots and aircrewmen use their superior judgement to avoid situations where they might have to use their superior skills.

If you do not know who the Marine Corps' greatest pilot (or crew chief, or gunner) is, it is not you.

While on your take-off roll, if an earthquake suddenly opens a 100 foot chasm across the runway and you crash into it, the mission of the Accident Board will be to find a way to blame it on pilot error.

Asking a Marine Corps pilot what he thinks of the FAA is like asking a dog what he thinks about fire hydrants.

Any twin engine aircraft doubles your chance of engine failure. And after one engine has failed, the most common purpose of your other engine is to fly you to the scene of your accident.

Aerial combat is the perfect vocation for men who want to feel like boys, but not for men who still are.

A tactic, done twice without crashing, becomes a procedure.

There are aviation *rules*, and there are aviation *laws*. The rules were made by men, and can be suspended. The laws (of physics) were made by The Deity, and should not be trifled with.

Any Marine pilot who relies on a "terminal forecast" can be sold the Brooklyn Bridge. Any Marine pilot who relies on a "winds aloft" report can be sold Niagara Falls.

Flying at night is almost as easy as flying in the daytime, because the airplane does not know that it is dark.

You can get *anywhere* in ten minutes if you fly fast enough.

But, you have *never* been lost until you are lost at Mach 2.

The two worst things that can happen to an old Marine Aviator:
  (1) One day you will walk out to your aircraft, knowing that it will be your last flight.
  (2) One day you will walk out to your aircraft, **not** knowing that it will be your last flight.

-- Admonitions for Marine Aviation --

When in doubt, climb! No one ever collided with the sky.

Remember, you can only *tie* the record for flying low.

If you absolutely must fly low, do not fly slow.

Marine Corps pilots and aircrewmen who hoot with the owls by night should not try to soar with the eagles by day.

Never, never, never forget your priorities! No matter how bad it gets, *fly the aircraft!* Fly it until the last piece stops moving. Remember: (1) aviate, (2) navigate, (3) communicate.

When the tanks are half empty, it is past time to review your plan.

Do not crash while trying to fly the radio. Aircraft fly because of the principle discovered by Bernoulli, not Marconi.

If a crash is inevitable, try to (1) strike the softest object in the vicinity, (2) as slowly and (3) as gently as possible.

When deviating from a rule, make your performance flawless (for example, if you fly under a bridge, try not to hit the bridge).

When flying VFR, stay out of the pretty little fluffy clouds, for mountains frequently lurk in them.

Plan ahead! Keep checking! If you find yourself on the ground or sitting in your rubber raft -- looking up in the sky where your aircraft used to be -- it is too late to check your fuel gauge.

Never let your aircraft take you somewhere your brain did not get to five minutes earlier. Remember that you fly your aircraft with your *brain*, not with your hands.

In a Marine Corps aircraft in flight, if something is (1) red, (2) yellow, or (3) dusty, never touch it without a lot of forethought.

In combat, remember that your aircraft is not a tank. Your windshield is not hi-tech plastic that bullets bounce off of.

Aircraft weight/temperature/altitude charts are *tools*. They are not *rules*. Play it safe and make *two* trips (helicopter crews, take note).

Before take-off always pause and ponder: "How much does all that Grunt stuff in the cabin *really* weigh?"

The two most crucial absolutes in Marine Aviation: (1) in airplanes, keep your airspeed up, and (2) in helicopters, keep your rotor RPM up. Otherwise, the Earth will rise up and smite thee.

If you enjoy life, watch your six (fighter pilots, take note).

When flying, Marine pilots should try to stay in the middle of the air. The edges of the air can be recognized by the appearance of trees, buildings, telephone poles, the ground, the sea, and mountains. It is very difficult to fly beyond the edges of the air.

Never forget the six most useless things in Marine Aviation:
1. The approach plates you did not bring.
2. The fuel you have burned.
3. The airspeed you had.
4. The altitude above you.
5. The runway behind you.
6. A tenth of a second ago.

Fighter and Attack pilots: When your fear of the aircraft exceeds your fear of the ejection seat, it is time to say goodbye.

In an emergency when you have run out of bright ideas, luck may be a perfectly acceptable substitute. But in the long run, trusting luck alone is not conducive to longevity.

In Marine Aviation you start with (1) a bag full of luck and (2) an empty bag of experience. The nifty trick is to fill your bag of experience before you empty your bag of luck.

Airspeed, Altitude, Brains. You need at least *two* at all times.

-- Ironies of Marine Aviation --

Combat *flying* is not dangerous. *Crashing* is what is dangerous.

Combat flying is not like a video game. When flying, you can not push a button and start over.

When flying in combat, being *good* and being *lucky* sometimes is still not good enough.

A thunderstorm usually is not quite as bad on the inside as it looks on the outside. It is worse.

In Marine Aviation, everything that goes up must come down. Going up is usually easy. It is the manner of *coming down* that can spoil your whole day.

In a crisis it is always better to (1) break ground and head into the wind, than to (2) break wind and head into the ground.

In a crisis it is always better to (1) be on the ground, wishing you were flying, than to (2) be flying, wishing you were on the ground.

The farther you fly over the mountains at night, the stronger the strange fuselage vibrations will become.

Day or night, the most crucial radio frequencies will be illegible.

Combat flight experience is something you never have enough of until *after* you desperately need it.

In retractable gear aircraft, if it takes over 80% power to taxi, you probably have landed gear-up.

There are three simple rules for making smooth landings, but no one knows what they are.

For pilots, (1) a smooth landing is mostly luck, (2) two in a row is all luck, and (3) three in a row is lying.

When flying, you are never lost if you do not care where you are.

In combat it is true that more aircraft are downed by a shortage of spare parts than by enemy fire. The big difference is that few Marine Aviators ever *die* because of a shortage of spare parts.

A competent pilot has mastered a host of complex skills. A competent aircrewman can perform myriad functions. Yet, none of these skills and functions guarantee survival in combat.

-- Infamous Military Aviation Predictions --

Heavier-than-air flying machines are impossible.
[Lord Kelvin, President of the Royal Society, 1895]

It is complete and utter nonsense to believe that flying machines will ever work.
[Sir Stanley Mosley, philosopher, 1905]

We soon saw that the helicopter had no future, so we dropped it. The helicopter does, with great labor, only what the balloon does without labor. The helicopter is no more fitted than the balloon for rapid horizontal flight. If its engine stops, it must fall with deathly violence, for it can neither glide like an aeroplane nor float like a balloon. The helicopter is easier to design than the aeroplane. But, it is utterly worthless!
  [Wilbur Wright, co-developer and pilot of the world's first successful airplane in 1903, writing in 1909]

We do not consider that aeroplanes will be of any possible use for war purposes.
[Report of the British Secretary of State for War, 1910]

Airplanes are interesting toys, but are of no military value.
[Marshall Ferdinand Foch, Professor of Strategy, 1911]

The aeroplane is an invention of the devil. It will never play any part in the defense of the nation, my boy!
[Sir Sam Hughes, Canadian Minister of Defence, 1914]

> "Aaaaahhh, sh--[an expletive]."
> [According to McDermott Associates (specialists in cockpit voice recorders), the most common *final words* on cockpit voice recorder tapes of airliners which have crashed. Usually voiced with resignation -- no emotion, no panic, no sarcasm. Basically an acknowledgement that all that could be done, had been done.]

Happy Hour Laws of Combat for Marine Helicopters

Marine Corps helicopters are *different*. They kill you *quickly*. No matter how good you are, no matter how lucky you are, no matter how much your mother loves you, a helicopter can kill you in the twinkling of an eye. The impending peril for helicopter crews and helicopter passengers was summed up by Harry Reasoner on *ABC Evening News* on 16 February 1971 when he stated:

A helicopter does not want to fly. It is maintained in the air by a variety of forces and controls working in opposition to each other. And if there is any disturbance in this delicate balance, the helicopter stops flying immediately and disastrously.

There is no such thing as a gliding helicopter. That is why being a helicopter pilot is so different from being an airplane pilot. Airplane pilots are open clear-eyed buoyant extroverts, and helicopter pilots are brooding introspective anticipators of trouble. They know that if something bad has not happened, it is about to.

A Marine Corps helicopter will kill you more quickly than any other instrument ever conceived by the mind of man. And in combat, helicopters fly to evil places where the enemy can kill you quickly, too. Therefore, pilots, crew chiefs, and gunners must *always remember* five things about flying in Marine helicopters:

1. In a helicopter, eternal vigilance is the price of survival.
2. There is no such thing as a gliding helicopter.
3. The safest helicopter is the one that can barely kill you.
4. You are always a student in a helicopter.
5. If at first you do not succeed, **never** try autorotations again.

Any Marine Warrior foolish enough to consider flying, or riding, in a helicopter should carefully study the following sub-chapters:

1. Philosophy for Marine Helicopters
2. Admonitions for Helicopter Crews
3. Rules for Learning to Fly Helicopters

-- Philosophy for Marine Helicopters --

Any mechanical contraption that attempts to *screw* its way into the sky is doomed to failure.

According to the laws of physics and aerodynamics, helicopters can not fly. They are just so ugly that the Earth repels them.

In helicopters the foreseeable future is the next five seconds. Long range planning is the next two minutes.

Marine Corps helicopters are tricky machines. Helicopter crews measure their lives in days, not years.

When your helicopter "wings" are leading and lagging, coning and flapping, sinister forces are at play.

The evil aerodynamic phenomena known as (1) Vortex Ring State, (2) Retreating Blade Stall, and (3) Power Settling are nothing more than fancy ways to describe instant death.

Helicopter crews fly with an intensity akin to *spring loaded* while waiting for pieces of their craft to fall off.

You can always identify a Marine helicopter crewman in a car, boat, or train. He (1) never smiles, he (2) listens to the machine, and he (3) always hears something he thinks is not quite right.

At any small airport there are lots of old airplanes lying around, but you *never* see an old helicopter -- *think* about it.

The terms *protective armor* and *helicopter* are mutually exclusive.

Whoever said "the pen is mightier than the sword" never flew in a Marine helicopter in a AAA and missile threat environment.

Repeatedly flying helicopters into a AAA and missile threat environment does not require only courage. It requires stupidity.

When (1) the weather is clear, (2) the rotors are in track, (3) the fuel tanks are full, and (4) all gauges are in the green, you are about to be surprised. That is just what helicopters do.

There are two types of combat aircraft, (1) fighters and (2) targets. Unfortunately a helicopter is not a fighter.

In fixed-wing aircraft, (1) airspeed is *life* and (2) altitude is *life insurance*. But in helicopters, rotor RPM is *everything!*

Sudden loud noises in a Marine Corps helicopter *will* get your undivided attention. This is especially true (1) at night, (2) while IFR, and (3) while over the mountains or ocean.

The three best things in life are (1) a good orgasm, (2) a good landing, and (3) a much needed bowel movement. For a helicopter crew, a successful return from an emergency night medevac is a unique opportunity to experience them all at the same time.

In combat there is no such thing as a *secure* LZ. Anyone who says otherwise is selling something.

On any medevac, the amount of time you must spend in the LZ is *directly* proportional to the intensity of enemy fire.

On emergency night medevacs, the LZ coordinates usually will be at the junction of several maps.

Among Marine helicopter crews after an emergency ammo resupply at night, the *first* liar does not stand a chance.

Flying is better than riding in a vehicle, which is better than running, which is better than walking, which is better than crawling -- all of which are better than an *emergency night medevac* under fire in a helicopter, although, *technically*, it is a form of flying.

Will Rogers never met a fighter pilot.

Fighter pilots make movies, but helicopter crews make history.

-- Admonitions for Helicopter Crews --

Marine Corps pilots and aircrewmen: helicopter time in your logbook is worse than S.T.D. in your Health Record.

Flying in a helicopter is about the same as masturbating. It *may* be fun at the time, but it is nothing to brag about in public.

Rotor RPM *must* be kept within the green arc. Failure to heed this admonition will adversely affect the morale of the crew.

When flying helicopters, the main trick is to keep the fuselage from turning as fast as the rotors.

If everything is working properly on your helicopter, consider yourself temporarily lucky.

When flying a Marine Corps helicopter, keep checking. There is always something you have missed.

Simultaneously running out of (1) airspeed, (2) altitude, (3) rotor RPM, (4) luck, and (5) bright ideas will ruin your day.

Running out of (1) collective, (2) pedal, (3) forward cyclic, or (4) aft cyclic are all exceptionally bad ideas.

If your engine fails you have 3/10 of a second to either (1) lower the collective, or (2) begin flying like a manhole cover.

In combat Marine Corps helicopter crews usually fly on a reactive basis. So, always (1) eat when you can, (2) sleep when you can, and (3) get in a good bowel movement when you can. Your next opportunity may not come around for a long, long time.

Flying a helicopter at an altitude in excess of 250 feet is considered risky and downright foolish.

If you ditch at sea in a helicopter, get out immediately. It will sink in 20 seconds (plus or minus about 19).

In combat it is, generally speaking, unwise to make an emergency helicopter landing in any enemy-infested area that our fixed-wing friends have recently bombed or strafed.

In a Marine Corps helicopter, *death* is the price you pay for trying to look Sierra Hotel.

Non-practitioners: ***never, never,*** sneak up behind an old helicopter pilot or aircrewman and clap your hands.

-- Rules for Learning to Fly Helicopters --

A few final words of wisdom for Marine Warriors who are non-practitioners in the helicopter world. You may be a fixed-wing pilot or aircrewman with an urge to expand your skills. Or you may be a Grunt, a professional population control specialist, with a dream of learning to fly helicopters.

No problem. If you can drive a car, why not try helicopters? Just follow these six simple easy-to-understand rules:

Rule 1: *Think* about it. Physicists, aerodynamic experts, and scientists have no idea what holds a helicopter up. But whatever it is, it could stop at any moment. Go to Rule 2.

Rule 2: After pondering the issue, in all probability you should forget the whole thing. If not, go to Rule 3.

Rule 3: In the helicopter, sit by someone who actually knows how to fly the thing. Let *him* fly it. Go to Rule 4.

Rule 4: In flight, when told to take the controls, **refuse!** (Hint: this is very important!) Do not *touch* anything. If you should *inadvertently* touch something, *do not move it.* Your options are: (A) Return to Rule 2. (B) If your life insurance premiums are current, you may go to Rule 5.

Rule 5: **Never, never,** let the pilot (the guy who knows how to fly the thing) demonstrate an **autorotation**. That is when you cut the engine off and drop like a pallet of bricks. It is sort of like *bungee jumping*, except that it is (A) straight down, (B) at warp speed, (C) with no bungee, and (D) you know you are going to die. Yet, if by virtue of some miracle or some act of Providence you *survive* the impact, go to Rule 6.

Rule 6: Return to Rule 2.

Landing In Trees: A power-off landing into a heavily wooded area should be accomplished by executing a normal autorotative approach and flare. The flare should be executed so as to reach zero rate-of-descent and zero ground speed as close to the tops of the trees as possible . . . .
  [**believe it or not**, a verbatim excerpt from Section 5-36, NATOPS Manual, CH-46D Helicopter]

Happy Hour Military Terms for Marine Infantry

Listen up! These military terms are used each day by the world's premier all-terrain combatants, the elite Marine Infantry. In other words, these terms are usually "Grunt stuff."

But, all you aviation types, do not forget that "every Marine a rifleman" concept. This Grunt stuff is important for you, too. Do you remember the official military definition of *Cranial-Rectal Inversion Syndrome*? *Combat Experience*? *Bravery*? How about *Scrounge*? Do you know the official definition of *Marriage*? *Mail Buoy Watch*? The *U.S. Navy*?

All of those terms are here, but they do not apply only to the Infantry. When Marines speak of Infantry and Aviation, there is no *them* or *they*. We are all U.S. Marines, all in the same Corps, the same Brotherhood. These terms apply to all Marine Warriors. Yet, they are absolutely, positively, need-to-know crucial stuff for all population control specialists, the Grunts.

Following this list is an *additional* list that is unique to Marine Aviation. All gung-ho Magnificent Grunt assassins ought to take a quick look at the aviation list, too. Yet, one note of caution! Grunts who read the aviation list more than twice will *never* agree to ride in a helicopter again:

AAV: A high-speed, hi-tech, souped-up AMTRAC.

Airman: (1) A flaccid civilian detainee in the U.S. Air Force. (2) A pitiful chair-borne public assistance program reject. (3) A useless person whose lack of initiative, intellect, and physical stamina renders him incapable of finding employment in the private sector. (4) A person often mistaken for an inner-city sanitation worker due to the common slovenliness of their attire.

ALICE: (1) In *theory*, a possible good-time companion on leave or liberty. (2) In *reality*, not much fun in the deep end of the pool.

Ammo Dump: A place you should avoid during incoming mortar, rocket, or artillery fire -- even if it is a deep hole.

Armored Vehicle: The catch-all name for any heavy mobile steel conveyance that attracts armor-piercing incendiary rounds.

Artillery: (1) Often called the *King of Battle*. (2) A weapon designed to kill or maim as many of the enemy and his evil cohorts as possible and restore cave-dwelling as an acceptable way of life in the former enemy territory. (3) Next to a Marine and his rifle, the most lethal weapon known to man.

Ashore: Anywhere in the air, on land, and sea -- except on base.

Ballistic: A characteristic of First Sergeants and Sergeants Major.

BAM: (1) The universally revered and respected military acronym for a gung-ho Woman Marine. (2) A fighting female warrior.

Bayonet: (1) A weapon of last resort. (2) A poor choice of weapons to use in a firefight (the guy with the *bullets* will win).

Bayonet Fighting Expert: A Marine Warrior who knows that the Vertical Buttstroke is not a sexual technique.

Beachhead: The guaranteed *bull's-eye* for enemy mortars, rockets, artillery fire, and aerial bombardment.

BLT: (1) A lethal Marine Corps force. (2) Something that can not be ordered in any restaurant.

Board of Inquiry: A spurious group of staff pogues who, given enough time and data, can prove anything.

Bravery: In common usage, a synonym for stupidity.

Brig: (1) A poor selection for lodging accommodations. (2) For macho Marine Warriors, an *even worse* selection if the rest of their unit is in combat.

Brown-bagger: (1) A Marine Warrior who has stumbled into the dark and thorny snake-pit of marriage. (2) A term derived from the small *brown paper lunch bag* carried by married warriors who can no longer afford to buy their own meals.

"Carry on": A verbal order which means *resume doing nothing*.

Casualty Assistance Officer: A staff pogue who, after the battle, will have a list upon which you hope your name is not included.

Chinese Fire Drill: A time consuming group endeavor noteworthy for its absence of coordination and purpose.

Cinderella Liberty: A devious and despicable staff pogue ruse designed to encourage sobriety among Marine Warriors.

Close: A near-miss, a matter of dire concern in the related arts of (1) horseshoe throwing and (2) grenade tossing.

Close Air Support: A good thing to have -- if it is not *too* close.

College Campus: Tragically, a place where pitiful apostles of "political correctness" outnumber men of principle and honor.

Combat: What you are definitely in when you have run out of everything except the bad guys.

Combat Breakfast: (1) Two aspirins, (2) two cups of coffee (if available), a (3) quick prayer, and a (4) quick puke.

Combat Experience: The sum of your combat mistakes.

Combat Pay: (1) A flawed concept. (2) A premise which allows the government to *save money* by temporarily paying you *more money* in anticipation of your expedited demise.

<u>Commandant's Professional Reading List</u>: A list of books that ***does not*** include (1) *Fighter Aces of the Iraqi Air Force* or (2) *Under Fire as a Combat Photographer*, by Albert "Al" Gore Jr.

<u>Communism</u>: (1) An ideology embraced by Marx, Engels, and other ignorami. (2) A form of socialism designed to impoverish any governmental entity. (3) A concept that would only work in Heaven, where it is not needed, and in Hell, where it is already established. (4) An easy way to raise suffering to a higher level.

<u>Computer</u>: (1) An electro-mechanical marvel, the operation of which is beyond the intelligence level of the intended user. (2) The primary cause of profanity among Marine Warriors.

<u>Conclusion</u>: Your best guess when you get tired of thinking.

<u>Corpsman</u>: In combat, a very good man to buddy-up with.

<u>Cranial-Rectal Inversion Syndrome</u>: (1) A debilitating U.S. Navy illness. (2) A progressive and degenerative malaise. (3) A chronic nautical paralysis believed by medical experts to result from a despicable U.S. Navy practice too uncouth to mention.

<u>Critical Terrain</u>: Terrain which, if not grabbed or camped out on, will make you the *screwee* in offensive or defensive warfare.

<u>D-Day</u>: The day before which your insurance documents and your *Last Will and Testament* should be completed.

<u>Death Before Dishonor</u>: The most popular tattoo among Marines.

<u>Defilade</u>: When the firing starts, the best position to be in.

<u>Demilitarized Zone</u>: A zone that should be, but usually is not.

<u>Devil Dog</u>: (see "Marine").

<u>Diplomacy</u>: The art of explaining to the bad guys the manner and certainty of their impending demise if they fail to surrender.

Drill Instructor: A maniacal, sadistic, extremist psychopath whose name you will never forget.

Field Day: A despised indoor non-athletic activity.

Field Scarf: An adornment worn on dress uniforms, but *never* worn in the field.

Fighting Hole: As the name implies, a Marine Warrior's *fighting* position (as opposed to an Army foxhole, a *hiding* position).

Flex: A really cool-sounding and non-doctrinal term to explain how your unit will maneuver, under fire, from one battlefield location to another, when no one has a clue.

Fool: A combatant who believes in fighting fair.

Forward Air Controller: (1) A "FAC," pronounced, *fack*. (2) An unfortunate former pilot. (3) A devious person who must be closely watched (Grunts interested in longevity should dive in a deep hole the instant their FAC begins chatting on his radio, for smoke and loud noise often follows).

Four-Wheel-Drive: A vehicle capability which enables one to get stuck in the mud at more remote and inaccessible locations.

Geneva Convention: A symposium of civilians who made up rules that warriors must follow in war -- unless no one is watching.

Good Judgement: Mental decision-making capacity derived from experience, which is derived from *bad* judgment.

Grunt: (see "Marine").

Guidebook for Marines: The most lyrical and inspirational literary creation in the post-revolutionary United States of America.

Gulf War: Four-day target practice in the land of sand, c 1991.

Gungy: An enlightened, surreal, euphoric, gung-ho state of mind.

H-Hour: The most introspective time of day.

Head: In times of utter confusion, the small room in which you *still* should know what you are doing.

Hero: The gungy illustrious term that all Marine Warriors apply to themselves (in the club after the fourth drink).

Heroism: A trait often displayed in combat after one has run out of all other viable options.

Hey-diddle-diddle: With reference to an assault, (1) words which describe an absence of analytical thought, or (2) an offensive warfare tactic which guarantees an 80% or higher casualty rate.

HMMWV, Humvee, Hummer, or whatever: The western world's most expensive four-wheel-drive military or civilian play-toy.

Hump: (1) As a *noun*, something you hope is short and downhill. (2) As a *verb*, the least preferred mode of personal transportation.

Jarhead: (see "Marine").

Junk on the Bunk: Your *things on the springs*.

LAV: (1) A small motorized conveyance with a big identity crisis. (2) A younger brother to a tank. (3) A thin-skinned steel box primarily useful as a crematorium for its occupants.

LCAC: (1) A huge 50-knot flying carpet. (2) A magical machine that defies gravity and all known laws of physics.

Leatherneck: (see "Marine").

LHA: The official military acronym for Luxury Hotel Afloat.

LST: The official military acronym for Little Slow Target.

<u>M-16A2 Rifle</u>: (1) A 5.56mm magazine fed, gas operated, air cooled, shoulder fired weapon that is always manufactured by the *lowest bidder*. (2) The original point-and-click interface.

<u>M-18A1 Claymore Mine</u>: A directional antipersonnel mine upon the side of which -- after deployment in combat -- you fervently hope you can not read the words, "Front, Toward Enemy."

<u>M-2 Bradley Fighting Vehicle</u>: (1) The most uncomfortable mode of mechanized transportation on Earth. (2) A thin skinned steel box (think, *target*) which should be avoided like the bubonic plague during a tank battle.

<u>M-203 Grenade Launcher</u>: A single shot, breech loaded, pump action, shoulder fired mini-bomb launcher, for which a tactical nuclear round would be an excellent idea.

<u>M-240G Machine Gun</u>: A heavy 7.6mm automatic weapon that you hope someone, *other than yourself*, has to carry.

<u>M-9 Service Pistol</u>: A firearm which -- if it is all you have in a firefight -- you **quickly** should exchange for a belt-fed weapon.

<u>Maggie's Drawers</u>: (1) For all red-blooded Marines, the only set of drawers they *never* want to see. (2) An embarrassing insult.

<u>Mail Buoy Watch</u>: (1) A crucial nocturnal assignment for all new and useless U.S. Navy ensigns. (2) An aquatic snipe hunt.

<u>Map</u>: An archaic land navigation aid which is totally useless on the modern-day battlefield (unless all of your batteries have died).

<u>Marine (the standard "Grunt" variant)</u>: (1) A professional assassin. (2) A minister of death, praying for war. (3) A population control specialist. (4) An indispensable element of the United States' Foreign Policy. (5) The only reason for the existence of Marine helicopters. (6) A revered warrior who will go anywhere at any time and destroy whatever he is ordered to destroy -- as long as he is allowed to sing obscene songs, kick cats, drink, brawl, embellish

war stories beyond recognition, and corrupt members of the opposite sex. (7) A member of the *gungy* group of misfits known as *Uncle Sam's Misguided Children.* (8) A warrior for whom all reading and writing test requirements have been waived and for whom "***Ooo-rah!***" is the proper response to any question from a superior. (see "Recon," "U.S. Marine Corps," and "Warrior")

Marriage: (1) Technically, not a military term. (2) A civil snake-pit into which well-intentioned Marines sometimes stumble. (3) The tragic result of trying to *think* with the wrong part of one's anatomy. (4) A progressive three-ring circus: engagement ring, wedding ring, and suffering. (5) The primary cause of divorce.

Medal: (1) The generic name for any one of the many gaudy uniform trinkets. (2) The shiny doo-dads that aggressive Marine Warriors always want more of -- *exclusive* of the Purple Heart.

MEU: Next to a Class 5 hurricane or a 700 foot high tsunami, the most lethal force on planet Earth.

MEU (SOC): A lethal force *more* destructive than a Class 5 hurricane or a 700 foot high tsunami.

Mine: The generic name for any Equal Opportunity Weapon.

Mortar: The weapon you would least like to hump into combat.

MOUT: (1) Exclusive of the north pole and south pole, the last environment on Earth in which U.S. Marines want to fight. (2) A battlefield where discretion *really* is the better part of valor.

MPC: (1) Funny-money. (2) As worthless as "Monopoly" money.

Napalm: (1) Incendi-gel. (2) An outstanding area support weapon.

Nomex: A synthetic fiber designed to burst into flame at moderate temperatures and be impossible to extinguish.

Ode to Naivety (posthumous): "Often wrong, but never in doubt."

<u>Old Corps, The</u>: (1) The bygone era when John Wayne was on active duty. (2) The era when the Chinese Army did not have enough rowboats to invade Taiwan.

"<u>Ooo-rah!</u>": For some mysterious reason, what Marine Warriors shout whenever they want to.

<u>Payback</u>: An inspirational experience *if* you survive it.

"<u>Peace is our Profession</u>": The pacifist motto (*really*, believe it or not) of the civilian-like U.S. Air Force.

<u>Perimeter Defense</u>: What Gen. George Armstrong Custer, USA, and his 7th Cavalry troopers should have established at the Little Big Horn on 25 June 1876, shortly before their untimely demise.

<u>PFM</u>: The military acronym for the comprehensive, easy-to-understand, non-technical explanation for why a complex system functioned as it did -- when no one has a clue.

<u>Pogey Bait</u>: (1) The most nutritious of the four major food groups. (2) The instant energy source of choice, especially when one's cholesterol level is too low.

<u>Political Correctness Counsellor</u>: (1) A civilian advisor who is depriving a village, somewhere, of its idiot. (2) A person who would be out of his depth in a parking lot puddle. (3) An utter ignoramus. (4) A wimp, a hand-wringing sniveling weakling.

<u>Preparation Fire</u>: (1) Commonly called *prep-fire*. (2) Smoke and loud noise designed to promote unwarranted confidence among members of the waiting assault force.

<u>Purple Heart</u>: The *least desirable* military medal awarded to Marine Warriors by the United States of America.

<u>R & R</u>: (1) In *theory*, the standard military acronym for "Rest and Recuperation." (2) In *reality*, usually "I & I."

Radio: When in a firefight, a useless electronic suggestion box.

Rate of Fire: (1) The *theoretical* number of rounds a weapon could fire in one minute. (2) A *meaningless* term, because the weapon would melt if any idiot tried to do it.

Recon: (1) The *stealth* version of the basic Marine Grunt. (2) A highly skilled and motivated population control specialist. (3) A warpainted Marine Warrior who prefers to fight with his Ka-Bar, bayonet, E-tool, and fists, just to conserve ammunition.

Reconnaissance by Fire: A noisy technique used on patrol when Marine Warriors can not see through the thick bushes.

REMF (spoken, *"ree-miff"*): The standard USMC acronym for Rear-Echelon-Mother-[expletive]. A derisive term used by U.S. Marine infantrymen and aircrews to describe military personnel in safe administrative and support roles, far from the fighting -- even though such persons are often secretly envied.

Roach Coach: A mobile, civilian-owned, mercenary distributor of diarrhea, heartburn, and other symptoms of gastrointestinal distress.

Rug Dance: (1) A rhythmic shuffling endeavor that requires no partner. (2) A spirited form of dancing during an extraordinarily one-sided chat with one's irate superior.

Rules of Engagement: The childish rules that you and your fellow warriors can *claim* you followed to the letter -- if you have killed all of the bad guys who might have claimed otherwise.

Sailor: (1) A primitive pre-Neanderthal life form. (2) A deck ape. (3) A nautical paint-picker. (4) A member of the under-class of dark, slimy, pitiful, squid-like creatures, most of whom have been banished to their natural habitat in the murky depths of the oceans where normal human beings do not have to associate with them.

Samsonite Luggage: The U.S. Air Force equivalent of a seabag.

Scrounge: (1) A *verb*; meaning to obtain by a devious method. (2) A *noun*; meaning a highly skilled U.S. Marine who is adept at obtaining, by devious methods, virtually anything from crates of frozen steaks to tactical atomic weapons. (3) A comshaw artist.

Secure: A term with differing implications. For example, if asked to *secure* a building, the following actions will be taken:

U.S. Navy: Turn out the lights and shut the door.

U.S. Air Force: Set up a three year lease with an option to buy.

U.S. Army: Occupy the structure, post a guard, and permit only persons with proper identification to enter.

U.S. Marine Corps: Target the building, call in an airstrike, and follow-up with heavy artillery. Complete the destruction with supporting arms. Conduct a *hey-diddle-diddle* assault to kill any possible survivors. Occupy the ruins. Fortify the position. Hold the ground at all costs, against all foes, until properly relieved.

Short-arm Inspection: A filthy despicable practice which has been rendered obsolete by the miracles of modern medicine.

Slopchute: (1) A geedunk that serves libations. (2) A facility not noted for stocking nutrients of the four major food groups.

Smoking Lamp: A nonexistent lamp that can, nonetheless, be *lit.*

SNAFU / FUBAR / SAPFU: Acronyms, not words, listed in ascending order of implied ineptitude and/or stupidity.

Snake and Nape: In a protracted firefight, a wonderful thing to discover that your Marine Air brothers have plenty of.

Sniper's motto: "Reach out and touch someone."

Soldier: The common name for a member of the U.S. Army, the bureaucracy which occupies former enemy territory that has been conquered by warriors of the U.S. Marine Corps. Soldiers in this administrative bureaucracy are recognized by (1) their trousers, which are too short; (2) their covers, which are too large; (3) the huge pockets on their clothing, in which they can warm their dainty little hands; and (4) the vast assortment of emblems, crests, badges, and shiny dangling doo-dads that adorn their dress uniform, which is similar in appearance to that of a Greyhound bus driver.

Straight Scoop: *Factual* information, as opposed to a new PFC saying, "I just got the word . . . ."

Stuff: A nebulous term that can refer to (1) a tangible thing, or to (2) a situation, condition, or process, as exemplified below:

A: *This is rough stuff.* Typical statement of an Air Force NCO while driving his air-conditioned sedan, from his air-conditioned office, to his air-conditioned quarters, **in the rain.**

B: *This is really rough stuff.* Typical statement of an Army Ranger, weapon at sling arms and carrying a 30 pound pack, after jumping from an aircraft and marching two miles to the *wrong* map coordinates, **in the rain.**

C: *This is horrible stuff.* Typical statement of a Navy SEAL, lying in the mud with his 60 pound pack, weapon in hand, after jumping from an aircraft, swimming two miles to shore, and crawling two miles to the *wrong* objective, **in the rain.**

D: *I love this stuff.* Typical statement of a camouflaged U.S. Marine Recon, up to his eyeballs in a vermin-infested swamp, with his 100 pound pack, a weapon in each hand; after jumping from an aircraft, swimming five miles to shore, killing several alligators while creeping ten miles through the swamp, attacking the enemy camp and slaying all occupants; and after slithering back into the slime of the swamp with plans to kill all enemy soldiers -- and all innocent civilians -- who wander past his undetectable vantage point, **in the rain.**

Sucking Chest Wound: Nature's way of telling you to slow down.

Supporting Fire: An excellent thing to witness *if* it is yours.

Surrender: A technique that Army soldiers often attempt to use, *especially* if they are into (1) masochism or (2) cold rice balls.

Tank: (1) A heavy steel box crammed full of high explosives. (2) An efficient crematorium for its talented crew. (3) Otherwise, a monument to the inaccuracy of direct fire.

Target of Opportunity: A bad thing to become, or be mistaken for.

Terrorist: A freedom fighter with a different perspective.

TRICARE: A *sick joke* on you and your family.

Tun Tavern: Where the world's best beer for warriors is brewed.

U.S. Air Force: (1) A government-funded amateur *flying club*. (2) An organization composed of prima donna aeronautical wannabes who were unable to find employment in the private sector.

U.S. Army: (1) A governmental *gun club*. (2) A bureaucracy that provides remedial training and free housing for prison parolees and Rambo wannabes who have been unable to cope with the day-to-day pressures of society.

U.S. Marine Corps: (1) *Valhalla* for elite warriors. (2) The most exclusive club on Earth. (3) The home of The Few, The Proud, and A Few Good Men. (4) The elite Brotherhood of Marines in which you *earn the title*, and then retain it forever. (5) The place where Chesty still lives. (6) Freedom's sword and shield against the forces of evil and tyranny. (7) The most revered and feared fighting machine the world has ever known.

U.S. Navy: The government-sponsored aquatic *cruise service* that is provided on-call for the convenience of Marine Warriors.

Vampire: The common term for either (1) a this-is-no-drill enemy weapon, or (2) a mythical Transylvanian blood-sucker.

<u>Vietnam</u>: A place where it *did too* get cold at night.

<u>Vietnam War</u>: A conflict in which hundreds of U.S. Marines earned medals for extraordinary valor in combat every day, and in which -- from time to time -- a few were actually awarded.

<u>War</u>: In general, the unfolding of miscalculations.

<u>Warrior</u>: (1) A street-legal assassin. (2) A romping, stomping, devil-may-care purveyor of death and destruction. (3) A rough, overbearing, self-centered psychopathic killer by day, lover by night, and drunkard by choice. (4) Someone who can curse for ten minutes without repeating a word. (5) One who knows that "Kill, sir!" is the right answer to any question. (6) One who thinks that "sodomy" and "politically correct" should fall into the same subchapter in the UCMJ.

Happy Hour Military Terms
for
Marine Aviation

Heads up, you USMC aviation types! If staying alive in combat is of interest to you, this is crucial scientific stuff.

Be forewarned! Even in peacetime Marine Corps aircraft have been known to develop some perverse and evil habits. They come unglued in flight. They run out of gas. They butt heads with mountains in the dark. All of these idiosyncrasies adversely affect the longevity of those who ride or fly courtesy of Marine Air. And, do not even *mention* helicopters! If our Grunt friends knew all that we know about helicopters, they would not *be* our friends.

In this chapter we will define the things that keep us alive (or kill us), such as *Gravity*, *Hydroplane*, and *Dead Reckoning*. Also, *Pucker Factor* is scientifically explained. Are you confused about the *Bang-Stare-Red Theory*? *Chicken Plate*? *Retreating Blade Stall*? If so, this section is for you.

OK, you Magnificent Grunts! Do you want insight into Marine Aviation, the most perilous mode of transportation on Earth? If so, read on. You may find that early retirement is not such a bad idea:

A-Model: (1) An underpowered experimental aircraft prototype. (2) A primitive contraption you should *never* ride or fly in.

Accident Investigation Board: *Six men* who take *six months* reviewing what the deceased crew did during the last **six seconds** of their lives (in the rain, at night, in the mountains, under fire).

Acey-Deucey: A competitive exercise designed to weed out any Marine pilots who lack the killer instinct necessary for combat.

ADF: An aircraft navigation instrument of last resort.

<u>Aeronautics</u>: (1) Neither an industry nor a science. (2) A miracle.

<u>Aircraft</u>: (1) The precursor of the Frisbee. (2) The generic name for any noisy heavier-than-air flying machine. (3) The most unreliable and most perilous mode of transportation on Earth.

<u>Aircraft Carrier</u>: The biggest, most expensive, slowest moving, most explosive-filled, and most lucrative ***bull's-eye*** on Earth.

<u>Aircraft of the U.S. Marine Corps</u>:

<u>AH-1W/Z Super Cobra</u>: (1) A primitive flying machine unable to adapt to *wheel* technology. (2) A mini-attack helicopter that added more rotor blades to *try* to look like an Apache. (3) The only Marine helicopter unable to carry more than two Marines.

<u>AV-8B Harrier</u>: (1) A jet VTOL/STOL attack aircraft with *illusions* of also being a fighter. (2) The world's greatest airshow aircraft. (3) An effective tool for converting Marine wives into Marine widows.

<u>A-6E Intruder</u>: A lethal and electronically enhanced flying gas tank equipped with one or two love-seats.

<u>CH-46E Sea Knight</u>: An antiquated, dilapidated helicopter known by its aircrew *survivors* as the "shuddering [expletive]." Just say a *Hail Mary* and climb aboard.

<u>CH-53E Sea Stallion</u>: Aerodynamic proof of the hypothesis that, if you glued enough engines onto it, even a brick could fly.

<u>F/A-18E/F Super Hornet</u>: A sleek supersonic machine primarily useful for enemy surface-to-air-missile (SAM) target practice.

<u>KC-130A/J Hercules</u>: An ageless flying machine which was (1) designed in the 1940s, (2) in service in the 1950s, and which is (3) still being ***built*** during the next century.

<u>MV-22 Osprey</u>: A hi-tech bird of *prey*, in which you *pray*.

UH-1N/Y Huey: A primeval *skid-mounted* machine designed in the previous millennium, before man's invention of *wheels*.

Air Medal: A military award bestowed upon Marine Corps pilots and aircrewmen who blunder into a perilous situation in combat and, through **dumb luck** alone, manage to survive.

Airspeed: Expressed in knots, the speed of an aircraft relative to the air mass through which it travels (deduct 30% when listening to Air Force pilots, Navy pilots, and REMFs).

Aft Pylon: On CH-46 helicopters, the flimsy rear portion of the fuselage with a historical penchant for vanishing in flight.

All-Weather Close Air Support: Superior and overwhelming aerial fire support for U.S. Marine Corps Infantry, available 24 hours a day *except* (1) during inclement weather, and (2) at night.

"Alpha-Mike-Foxtrot": The common verbal farewell (1) to any despicable person, or (2) to an enemy you have just shot down.

Alternate Airport: Any airport 50 or more miles beyond the maximum range of a Marine Corps aircraft flying IFR.

Altimeter: A barometric pressure sensing device that indicates height above *sea level* (consequently, it is useless over *land*).

    Radar Altimeter: (1) Better than the plain altimeter. (2) An electronic sensing device that indicates height above either the land or the sea (3) Normally works OK -- unless you are flying IFR toward the side of a mountain.

Attitude Indicator: A cockpit instrument that had *better be working* while flying IFR or flying at night.

Autorotation: An inexplicable and terrifying helicopter maneuver that you only get *one chance* to try. Ironically, the higher you are when the terror begins, the better. (Also, see "Pucker Factor.")

<u>Back Side of the Power Curve</u>: (1) A dreaded world of *slow flight* defined by obscure laws of aerodynamics and physics that no one understands. (2) The side of the curve you do not want to be on.

<u>Bang-Stare-Red Theory</u>: A time-tested aeronautical truth which substantiates that (1) the louder a sudden *bang* in an aircraft, the quicker the pilot's eyes will be drawn to the gauges, and (2) the longer the pilot stares at the gauges, the quicker the needles will move from the green arcs into the red arcs.

<u>Bank</u>: The generic name for all civilian institutions that hold the liens on cars owned by Marine pilots and aircrewmen.

<u>Barrel Roll</u>: The preferred method of moving beer containers.

<u>Carburetor Icing</u>: In piston-powered manned aircraft and UAVs, a phenomenon which occurs when the fuel tanks mysteriously become full of air. (Also, see "Engine Failure.")

<u>CAVU</u>: (1) What aeronautical dreams are made of. (2) What Heaven surely must be like.

<u>Chicken Plate</u>: (1) Combat attire for U.S. Marine Corps helicopter crews. (2) Something that can not be ordered in a restaurant.

<u>Chip Detector Light</u>: A *really* evil thing when you are flying IFR.

<u>Cloud</u>: A beautiful fluffy opaque meteorological phenomenon in which mountains frequently lurk.

<u>Cluster Bombing</u>: An aerial bombardment technique. (Note: U.S. Air Force studies suggest that cluster bombing is 100% accurate, because their bombs *always* hit the ground.)

<u>Combat, Aerial</u>: What you are in when those pretty little *orange baseballs* are zipping past, and sometimes through, your aircraft.

<u>Copilot</u>: A useless crewmember *until* he spots closing traffic at 12 o'clock (after which he is an ignoramus for not seeing it sooner).

<u>Crab</u>: The squadron Operations Officer.

<u>Crash</u>: Nature's subtle way of warning Marine Corps pilots and aircrewmen to watch their airspeed.

<u>Cruise Box</u>: (1) A large footlocker that is loaded aboard a Marine Corps aircraft by its crew chief. (2) A useless heavy box, the weight of which reduces the passenger load by two Grunts.

<u>Dead Reckoning</u>: (1) You reckon correctly, or you are. (2) The least preferred method of aerial navigation.

<u>Drag</u>: A grossly intoxicated male aviator who has left the bar in a drunken stupor while wearing a woman's coat by mistake.

<u>Emergency Night Medevac (by helicopter)</u>: Either (1) a nocturnal emergency flight to save the life of a wounded Marine Warrior, or (2) a guaranteed cure for constipation, or (3) both.

<u>Emergency Recon Extraction</u>: (1) What Marine helicopter crews do in combat -- usually at night, for some obscure reason. (2) A sure remedy for "tired blood" or constipation.

<u>Engine Failure</u>: A phenomenon which occurs when the fuel tanks of an aircraft become full of air. (see "Carburetor Icing")

<u>Experienced Crew</u>: An aircraft crew that has survived long enough to recognize a mistake when they make it again.

<u>FAA motto</u>: "We are not happy until you are not happy."

<u>Famous Last Words (above and beyond all others)</u>: "Don't worry about the weight, it'll fly."

<u>Firewall</u>: In all Marine Corps aircraft, the metallic panel designed to direct flame and smoke into the cockpit.

<u>Flying</u>: (1) Something difficult to do without feathers. (2) The common term for the illusion of immortality. (3) The ability to

throw yourself through the sky and avoid hitting the ground.

Night Flying: Almost the same thing as *day* flying, except that you can not see where you are going.

FOD-Burger: An inedible substance, the ingestion of which will hopefully be discovered *prior* to attempted flight.

Fuel: A limited resource without which the U.S. Marines in an aircraft (1) become pedestrians, or (2) become deceased.

G-Suit: Clothing designed to prevent inappropriate aerial napping.

Glide Distance: Half the distance from a Marine Corps aircraft in distress to the nearest suitable emergency landing area.

GPS: (1) The aviation acronym for "Going Perfectly Straight." (2) Also, the common name of the electronic black box gizmo that enables you to "go perfectly straight."

Gravity: The primary cause of most Marine Corps aircraft crashes. It may not be fair, but (1) it is the law, (2) it is not subject to repeal, and (3) it is forever.

Headwind: (1) The result of any attempt to stretch fuel. (2) A meteorological occurrence on all lengthy over-water flights.

Helicopter: The common term for a complex, heavier-than-air, vertical takeoff, flying machine comprised of thousands of parts, all of which move in opposite directions, constantly striving to tear themselves apart, and often succeeding.

HIGE: The best place for a helicopter crew to hover.

HOGE: (1) An exceptionally stupid thing for a helicopter crew to do. (2) An invisible and mystical aerodynamic capability that helicopter crews **always** want to have, but **never** want to use.

Hover: A quasi-flying technique practiced by helicopter crews that have no specific place to go.

Hydroplane: A flying machine designed to land on wet runways.

IFR: (1) In common day-to-day usage, an acronym for "I follow railroads." (2) Otherwise, a tricky method of flying by needle and horoscope. (3) Not nearly as much fun as simple VFR.

Instrument Flying: (1) An unnatural act. (2) Not a good idea. (3) How you fly when you can not fly like you want to fly.

Jet Aircraft: The most expensive way to convert JP-8 into noise.

Landing: A technique for falling out of the sky with style.

> *Good* Landing: A landing after which all of the aircraft crewmembers can walk away without assistance.

> *Great* Landing: A landing after which (1) the aircraft doors will still open, and (2) the aircraft can be salvaged.

Landing Gear Handle: The cockpit handle that a smart pilot will lower to the *down* position immediately after a gear-up landing.

Lean Mixture: Non-alcoholic beer.

> *Rich* Mixture: The type of beverage you order at the *other guy's* promotion party.

MARCAD: A wartime Marine Corps flight training program designed to produce (1) *twice* the pilot, at (2) *half* the price.

"Mayday! Mayday! Mayday!": A verbal notice that prayer, while it may not help, is probably an excellent idea.

Meatball: (1) A longevity-related phenomenon to be watched, not eaten. (2) A wonderful thing to see when flying on fumes.

Mile High Club: (1) If you do not know, you are not in it. (2) A club that requires a co-conspirator of the opposite sex.

Minimums: After crashing and surviving, the altitude below which you must swear you did not descend while flying IFR.

Nanosecond: The time delay built into stall warning systems.

Navigation, Aerial: The scientific process used by an aircrew to get from Point A to Point C, while *trying* to get to Point B.

OBE: The untenable mental condition that occurs when an aircraft travels faster than the brain of its pilot.

Pilot: A confused person who (1) talks about women when he is flying, and who (2) talks about flying when he is with a woman.

Precision Bombing: Hi-tech and smart weapon aerial bombardment accurate to within plus/minus seven miles -- more or less.

Preflight Planning: A time consuming exercise in futility.

Pucker Factor: (1) The precise formula (**T** x **I** x **R** over **H**) which determines the contraction force of the Gluteus Maximus muscles. (2) The common term for the *force of contraction* of these muscles in times of dire peril. (3) The scientific mathematical calculation which determines the *percentage* of seat cushion which will be sucked into the rectum of pilots and aircrewmen who are under enemy fire. On a 1-to-100 scale, the percentage may be calculated as follows: **T** (number of ***tracers*** headed your way) x **I** (your ***interest*** in staying alive, on a 1 to 10 ascending scale) x **R** (your ***rate*** of descent, in feet-per-minute) divided by **H** (your ***height*** above ground, in feet). Note: for mathematical computations, each incoming *missile* equates to *ten* tracers.

Question, Aeronautical: An inquiry directly related to flight, or a request for aeronautical clarification; for example: "Sir, was that a landing, or were we shot down?"

Range: For pre-flight planning purposes, the distance 20 to 30 miles beyond the point where all fuel tanks will become full of air.

Retreating Blade Stall: (1) The aerodynamic nemesis of helicopters that fly too fast before crashing. (2) Something *really* repulsive. (3) The primary cause of insomnia among helicopter crewmen.

"Roger": The radio transmission used by all pilots who are unsure of the proper radio response.

Roll: A design priority for all transport helicopters.

Running takeoff: A nifty practice maneuver. But if a helicopter *has* to do it, you do not want to be riding in it.

SAR: The type of mission you hope you are not the objective of.

Separation: The condition achieved when two or more aircraft fail to collide in flight.

"Sierra-Hotel": (1) What you say in correspondence, or in mixed company, when you can not say what you *really* want to say. (2) The socially appropriate but "politically incorrect" synonym for: Outstanding! Aggressive! Exemplary! Supremely skilled!

Single engine capability: At reduced speed, a level flight capability which most aircraft have -- *until* they try to land.

Slip: A flimsy civilian-style undergarment worn by some women.

Spoilers: The members of the Accident Investigation Board.

Stall: A technique for thwarting proposals of matrimony.

Tail Rotor: (1) The rear rotor on a helicopter which, despite the best efforts of the crew, is magnetically drawn toward trees, stumps, poles, wires, buildings, and other obstructions to flight. (2) The fragile and delicate little rotor that -- unlike the main rotor, which can chop down hickory trees -- will self-destruct if it hits anything bigger than a honey-bee.

<u>Tail Wind</u>: The result of eating beans and other leguminous foods.

<u>Terminal Forecast</u>: A complex horoscope with lots of numbers.

<u>Thunderstorm</u>: (1) The common term for *cumulo-securus* clouds. (2) Mother Nature's way of saying, "Up yours!"

<u>Translational Lift</u>: (1) For helicopter crews, a *very* good thing. (2) A phenomenon attributed to black magic.   (3) An aerodynamic wonderland that vanishes, unfortunately, when you try to land.

<u>Turn and Slip Indicator</u>: A cockpit instrument of no use to pilots.

<u>Useful Load</u>: The total volummetric capacity of a Marine Corps aircraft, regardless of weight.

<u>VFR</u>: (1) The meteorological conditions under which members of an aircrew can see what they collided with. (2) The rules that a pilot may "declare" if the mandated *IFR* procedure is too complex.

   Special <u>VFR</u>: Even more simple than *regular* VFR.

<u>Weather</u>: Next to *gravity*, the biggest cause of aircraft crashes.

<u>"What?"</u>: During flight, a question more important than "Why?"

<u>"Whiskey-Tango-Foxtrot?"</u>: (1) A *polite* radio or ICS query. (2) An in-flight question most often voiced when the crew of another aircraft is engaged in exceptionally stupid conduct.

   Do not spin this aeroplane!   If this aeroplane enters a spin, it will return to earth without further attention on the part of the aeronaut.
   [*Flying Manual*, Wright "B" Military Flyer, 1911]

About the Author

Marion Sturkey entered the Brotherhood of Marines in 1961. As a Captain, a helicopter pilot with combat experience in Vietnam, he left the Corps in 1968. Or, so he thought.

As the years passed, Marion discovered that no one ever truly leaves the Corps. He found that there is no such thing as an ex-Marine or a former-Marine. He learned that once it has been earned, the title, United States Marine, lasts for a lifetime.

After two non-military books, in 1996 Marion completed the professional *BONNIE-SUE: A Marine Corps Helicopter Squadron in Vietnam.* This true saga of commitment and sacrifice, love and brotherhood, has been reprinted time after time. Today it remains a military classic in both print and audiobook formats.

In 2002 Marion authored and published his fourth book, the up-beat and gung-ho *Warrior Culture of the U.S. Marines.*

A year later he published his fifth book, his first venture into the military satire genera, *Murphy's Laws of Combat.* It is often called, "the American Warrior's guide to 'staying alive' in battle."

Marion now lives in his original hometown, the idyllic rural *metropolis* of Plum Branch, South Carolina.

This **second edition** of *Warrior Culture of the U.S. Marines* fills a need to add material and update the original. Totally revised, it offers an up-to-date look at the elite Marine Warriors and their Corps.

Index

Semper Fidelis